To Be a Warrior

TO BE A WARRIOR

The Adventurous Life and
Mysterious Death of Billy Davidson

BRANDON PULLAN

RMB

For information on purchasing bulk quantities of this book, or to obtain
media excerpts or invite the author to speak at an event, please visit
rmbooks.com and select the "Contact" tab.

RMB | Rocky Mountain Books Ltd.
rmbooks.com
@rmbooks
facebook.com/rmbooks

Cataloguing data available from Library and Archives Canada
ISBN 9781771604376 (softcover)
ISBN 9781771604383 (electronic)

Interior design by Colin Parks

Printed and bound in Canada

We would like to also take this opportunity to acknowledge the traditional territories upon which we live and work. In Calgary, Alberta, we
acknowledge the Niitsítapi (Blackfoot) and the people of the Treaty 7
region in Southern Alberta, which includes the Siksika, the Piikuni, the
Kainai, the Tsuut'ina, and the Stoney Nakoda First Nations, including
Chiniki, Bearpaw, and Wesley First Nations. The City of Calgary is also
home to Métis Nation of Alberta, Region III. In Victoria, British Columbia,
we acknowledge the traditional territories of the Lkwungen (Esquimalt
and Songhees), Malahat, Pacheedaht, Scia'new, T'Sou-ke, and W̱SÁNEĆ
(Pauquachin, Tsartlip, Tsawout, Tseycum) peoples.

We acknowledge the financial support of the Government of Canada
through the Canada Book Fund and the Canada Council for the Arts, and
of the province of British Columbia through the British Columbia Arts
Council and the Book Publishing Tax Credit.

Disclaimer
The views expressed in this book are those of the author and do not neces-
sarily reflect those of the publishing company, its staff, or its affiliates.

FOR WESTERLY

CONTENTS

Ascending

Raised by government
And domestic tragedy
Bill climbed up and out
Past mountains of resistance
Seeking and laying a path
Ascending through recognition
Of his own unique route.

Shying from the fame
Of notable rockface climbers
He launched
Paddle in hand
Provisioned for time enough
To learn
The truth and splendor
Of personal independence
Entwining himself to earth and sea.

His perspective
Ethereal and grounded
Recognized and envied
By those who wish
But can not follow
He lived
Where heaven and earth collide
Becoming once
Again and gone.

—BRUCE MCMORRAN

PREFACE

It is easier to sail many thousand miles through cold and
storm and cannibals... than it is to explore the private sea,
the Atlantic and Pacific Ocean of one's being alone.
—*HENRY DAVID THOREAU*

ON MY FIRST VISIT TO THE CANADIAN ROCKIES, IN
2000, I picked up a copy of *Pushing the Limits* by Chic
Scott — a hardcover chronology of the most important climbs and climbers in Canada. I read it at night by
headlamp, lying in the back of my truck after long days
of climbing. Hundreds of climbers were mentioned in its
more than 400 pages, which had been compiled by Chic
during a cross-country hitchhiking adventure. The chapter
called "Canadian Mountaineering Comes of Age 1951–
1990" was the most interesting to me because it detailed
the history of technical rock and alpine climbing on some
of Canada's most difficult peaks. There were many characters who risked life and limb on dangerous rock climbs,
but one climber caught my attention more than most: Billy
Davidson. He was given four pages while other climbers got
only a paragraph or two. Chic wrote in great depth about
Billy's achievements, noting that as quickly as Billy came
into the Calgary climbing scene, he left.

I attended Lakehead University in Thunder Bay until 2004, and during that time I made seasonal trips to the Rockies and the west coast for climbing. I grew up listening to stories from my grandfather about his adventures as a young man and appreciated nothing more about an area than its history, so during my visits I made an effort to meet the people in Chic's book. Thanks to a few key people, it wasn't too hard to track down the most legendary climbers, even though it was before social media.

On Christmas Day 2005, I met Chic and pioneer ice climbers Jack Firth and Gerry Rogan. I was 25, had just moved to the Bow Valley and wanted to learn as much as I could about the history of climbing — the unwritten history. Joined by my climbing partner Danny O'Farrell, I sat with Chic, Jack and Gerry to drink Guinness and listen to stories. At some point during the evening, I asked how I could meet Billy. Chic told me that he had died the previous year by suicide or murder. If I wanted to know more about Billy, I would have to visit a climber in Calgary named Urs Kallen, one of Billy's best friends.

A few weeks later, I was knocking on the door of Urs's home in the city's northeast. I was standing next to my other climbing partner, Will Meinen. Urs answered the door with his wife, Gerda, and welcomed us into their home. The Swiss grandparents had prepared a dish of raclette, uncorked a bottle of Okanagan Valley wine and told Will and I that they were preparing an Alberta beef steak dinner for us. Urs, who I'd later find out was close friends with many famous climbers, like Alex Huber, Dean Potter, Beth Rodden and John Bachar, was happy we were visiting. That evening of stories and conversations forever changed my life and put it on the path it's on now. Urs told me that he would one day share more about Billy, but first I would have to write a book for him called *The Bold and Cold*. In 2016, that book, which tells the stories from 25 classic Canadian Rockies routes, was published. It was time to turn my attention back to Billy, so I drove back to Calgary and knocked on Urs's door.

When people asked me why I was researching Billy, I told them that Billy was an orphan who became one of the most important Canadian climbers ever, then became a hermit who lived off the land. He rewrote the book of what was possible in a kayak on the Pacific Ocean, and painted accurate bird's-eye-view water-colours of coastal shorelines. He kept articulate notes and journals. Over the years of piecing his adventures together, I wondered if he left all of those bread crumbs for someone like me to find, or if he had some ultimate goal of one day sitting down to write his own book.

While Billy kept excellent records of his climbs, paddling expeditions and travels, there are decades when he either didn't write anything down or his notes went missing. On one occasion, friends of his acci-dentally threw away hundreds of pages of his journals. Nevertheless, as much as Billy was a hermit, he made lifelong friends wherever he settled, and was a father. I've had the good fortune to meet many of his friends and family, from his childhood friend Perry Davis to his climbing partner Urs Kallen to his son, Westerly, and painter Stewart Marshall. I've also met a number of paddlers who came to idolize Billy's west coast lifestyle. Their journeys helped me better understand Billy's later years.

Over the past 15 years, I've climbed the vertical rock walls where Billy made a name for himself, hiked to the remote corners of the Rockies where he lived off the land and paddled on choppy Pacific Ocean waters where he fearlessly travelled long distances, alone. Since that Christmas Day with Chic, I've been looking for Billy Davidson, and although I never met him, I've included what I found in this book. It's only a small insight into his amazing life; some people didn't share their stories, and Billy had years' worth of solo adventures that only he knew about. Despite many conflicting reports and stories from his friends and partners — 40 years is a long time to remember details — I tried my best to weave the timeline between Billy's journals from his first climb as a 12-year-old to his last journal entry. While the events, climbs, paddles, camps, journals, letters and travels are all true, some specifics might vary depending on who you talk to. Ultimately, I hope that Billy's life of epic journeys leaves everyone inspired to go for an adventure, alone and with a journal.

Chapter 1

BILLY'S LAST DAY

Far out man, it's good to see a letter from your hand sent
to me. I'm off my rocker and to the northwest coast. I mean
to stop there for two weeks at the most. It's a fifty-mile
wonder upon rocks and sand, I've never seen such incred-
ible land. And when I get back to where I started today, I'll
take a crack at getting over your way.
—*BILLY DAVIDSON, LETTER TO ROB WOOD,*
March 5, 1975

THE FAMILIAR SMELL OF EULACHON OIL ROSE from the fire and clouded the air under the makeshift roof of Billy's camp. The northwest breeze pushed the smoke towards the water. Breakfast was cooking. The rising tide hid the exposed rocky shore, and a curious sea lion poked its head up from a shallow bay. Mew gulls flew overhead; they knew that Billy might have a fresh fish to fillet — head and guts. Billy wore his wool sweater, the one singed at the cuffs from handling pans on the grill. The flour darkened and the fire simmered. Billy sat on a log close to the fire; too close, he knew, and he would be smoked out, but too far and the heat wouldn't dry his damp clothes. Not that his clothes ever dried.

Billy reached down next to the log and picked up a stained yellow bag. Inside the smudged plastic wrapping was a small pouch of rolling papers with a drawing of a bearded man in a toque, smoking. Billy rolled his morning Drum and flipped the browning chapatis. He poured coffee into his metal cup, and with a tightly rolled cigarette hanging from his grey whiskers, had a sip. The fog that had hung close to the ocean over the previous days had lifted. Hail started to fall but turned to rain as Billy finished his coffee.

Gosling Island is one of many that make up the Goose Islands, where Billy had first camped back in the early 1990s. Gosling itself is mostly flat, unlike some of the mountainous islands on the horizon. It doesn't have small lakes like the larger Goose Island (for which the group is named) and is covered with evergreen trees. On his early forays, Billy established a camp on Duck Island, southwest of Goose, home to the Werkinellek 11 reserve, which belongs to the Heiltsuk First Nation and was once a seasonal harvesting village. In the 1800s, the Heiltsuk would travel there from Bella Bella for their annual spring seal hunt. More than once, Billy found his camp trashed; the Heiltsuk didn't like him camping there. So he moved his camp to Gosling.

The Goose Islands had seen little recreational boat traffic when Billy first visited, nearly 30 years earlier. The area had since become more popular for hunting and fishing in the summer, but was still quiet in winter. Billy's camp on Gosling was the culmination of decades of experience living off the land. It was one of dozens he'd established since first exploring the Inside Passage in the mid-1970s. Built in a sheltered forest above a beach in a small bay, it was protected by two blue tarps and had a wood reserve, a driftwood windscreen and a fire stand. A whisk hung from a branch that he would use to make chapatis, a dietary staple made of nothing more than sea water, seal oil and flour.

A few days earlier, Billy had gone hunting at the south point. He saw a deer eating close to the water's edge, but it was too big for him to be bothered with. Knowing that the December rains would get worse, he planned to hike to the west side of the island to his usual hunting ground to find smaller game. At 57, Billy found the hike longer than when he'd first made it years before. With his long knife sheathed and his shotgun on his shoulder, he made the trek with short glimpses of the sun. Throwing back his rain-jacket hood, he paused in small clearings to enjoy the warmth. His breath moved through the trees like a thick morning fog. The clouds drifted with the wind as the sun disappeared. Billy reached the west coast of Gosling. It was a rising tide, and the trees were close to the water. With little room to manoeuvre, he slipped on moss-covered logs. With no warning, big waves crashed to shore. And as dark clouds settled on the treetops, the light rain became hail once again. Billy returned to camp, empty-handed.

Under the tarped roof and next to the fire, he was mostly removed from the elements. He had been on the island for nearly a month, one-third of his planned trip. Next to him was a journal. He wrote in it every day, habitually, about wind direction, rain and tides. He'd been keeping track of his life since the mid-1960s. Many of his journals went missing over the years, but a few survived. The one he was using on Gosling was a square calendar book from the Wilderness Committee, every page a month of the year. Atop November was a photo of a woodland caribou with the caption "Hunting, both illegal and legal, and predation by wolves is also negatively impacting this remote population."

Billy's journals from past years were sometimes very meticulous. He'd record every meaningful event and new encounter and whether he'd painted or read. Some of his reports mentioned how many candles and lighters, of which colours, he had left for the trip, how much garlic powder was left, how many pouches of Drum were left, what animals and bugs were around, what he ate, when and where the moon and sun set or rose, the water level, how many mice were in his camp, how many mice he killed, how good his poos were, the tides, how much firewood he had and more. But his current journal didn't allow for long stories about the day, only point-form, mostly abbreviated notes.

He arrived on Gosling in the evening of November 7, 2003, with plans to stay for three months. He left Denny Island early in the morning that day and paddled south against a rising tide in the Hunter Channel. The northwesterly winds pushed waves against the portside of *Ayak*, Billy's kayak, making for a rough journey. After passing through the Prince Group to Queens Sound, he beached *Ayak* at sunset. He recorded, "Landed at twilight (bushed.)" Billy found his camp had been used and his water seep wasn't working.

For the next month, there would be strong winds and showers. The days after he arrived were used for bringing everything at camp back up to his standard. On his second day, an old wooden boat stopped near the beach, and he found otter tracks near his seep. The following day, a skiff with three hunters stopped nearby. Billy didn't pay it much attention. He stayed busy building a trail to a beach on the southern tip of the island. Another two hunters stopped on the 20th for a chat. On that same day, Billy noted that he was on his 11th pouch of Drum. A week later, Billy found a dead deer near a creek as he worked clearing brush. He wore heavy rain gear all day. That night, he repaired a rip in his rain pants.

The day after his hike to the west, he wrote in his journal about the overcast skies, light rain and moderate to strong east to southeast winds. At the bottom of the report, he wrote: "Lower back and stomach pains." On Sunday, December 7, 2003, he made what would be his last entry, noting that he was down to his sixth pouch of Drum. Conditions were "overcast with light rain showers and light and variable winds. Fog and drizzle with light north to northwest winds by noon." The weather report for the area was "6.1°C with north/northwest winds at 11kt gusting to 24kt."

He left a small dash beneath these last words, implying he had more to write, maybe about the moon or what he ate for dinner. The only visible difference between that journal entry and those of the previous few days was more space between the letters and lines. It was the last thing Billy ever wrote.

Three months later, Billy was found dead near his camp. He died by gunshot wound to the head. The RCMP gave Billy's personal items to Westerly, his son. Westerly's mother, Lori Anderson, recalls:

> What the RCMP told me about the discovery of Bill
> is that one of the older Indigenous fishermen who
> used to go out every now and again to take Billy a
> loaf of bread found his camp unattended; like he was

still there, but not. He went back to Bella Bella and reported it to the police, who went out and had a look. They were about to give up looking when they found Billy above the high-water mark, covered in flotsam, his rifle nearby. One boot on, one boot off. They figured based on decomposition that his time of death was in February/March. That is the part that doesn't make sense, his last journal entry was midday on December 7.

Billy suffered from severe toothaches during his final years, one of the most common causes of suicide throughout history. He was a renowned painter who, like Vincent van Gogh, used colours like cadmium yellow and red, which are high in lead. One theory is that Van Gogh suffered from lead poisoning and committed suicide by shooting himself in the stomach.

"Stewart Marshall, Billy's friend and painting mentor, told me that a lot of the Indigenous youth didn't like Bill hanging out on their land and living like their ancestors," said Lori. "He said they would sometimes go out and taunt Bill, firing guns over his camp, trying to scare him off." And for some reason, the RCMP said Billy's kayak was too damaged to recover, but Lori demanded they retrieve it. "It was perfectly fine other than a bit of sand," said Lori. "His jigger was still lashed to the top deck. A friend of ours from Sointula was up in the area fishing, and he agreed to pick up the kayak from Shearwater and bring it down to Sointula, which is where it remains, at Stewart Marshall's."

Then there was the man who Billy had physically harmed over 20 years prior, to save Lori from abuse at the logging camp where she'd lived. Around the same time as Billy made his final journal entry, Lori saw a man in a boat heading north from Quadra Island, and "as far as I could tell from the distance, it was him. "It looked like maybe a ten-foot clinker type. I have no idea about that boat or who was in it, but the memory gives me shudders."

Who ended Billy's life remains a mystery. Lori admits that her own shreds of memory might mislead her: "Grief coupled with imagination can be dangerous. You start remembering stuff and trying to piece things together whether they fit or don't fit."

Chapter 2

WOOD'S CHRISTIAN HOME

Twenty years from now you will be more disappointed by
the things that you didn't do than by the ones you did do.
So, throw off the bowlines. Sail away from the safe harbor.
Catch the trade winds in your sails.
—*MARK TWAIN*

BILLY WAS SIX YEARS OLD WHEN HIS MOM
opened the car door and walked him, his brother, Ken,
and his sisters to Wood's Christian Home, a shelter
for disadvantaged children in the old Hextall mansion
near the Bow River in Calgary's Bowness. Under cedar
shingles, stairs led up past a fieldstone foundation to
an open door. That would be the last time any of the
children saw their young mother. The year was 1953.

They were left standing in a Tudor-style room with
fancy furniture. There were around 100 other children
in the home, along with cooks, supervisors and matrons.
Some of the children were wards of the province, and
the home received one dollar a day for their care. A
letter soliciting donations was delivered to Calgarians,
showing an image of a ragged, helpless-looking child,
but the children came from every possible background.

A boy named Frankie Dwyer had already been at the home for seven years. His father, Francis Dwyer, had been caring for him at a Calgary flop house. Frankie never knew his mother, Annie McGowan. Frankie said a knife fight at the flop house forced his father to drop him off at Wood's Christian Home. "At the end we walked a long way, Dad wearing a long coat and a fedora," Frankie told me. "That was the fashion, and it was cold. We walked through gates and up a long, cin- der-coated drive to an immense house." Frankie wrote a book about his experience at Wood's called *Passing Innocence*, in which he wrote, "Sometimes fragments surface, quite vividly, and visit with me in the small hours of the night." He told me Wood's was a happy place, boisterous and spirited. "We were like an island. The other boys in Calgary were afraid of us. Our hockey team was legendary; we were tough kids."

The younger boys slept in a sunroom that had once been a tuberculosis sanatorium, which "was freaking cold," according to Frankie. "It was called the little boys' end. Next to it was the Oak Room, which the little boys had to cross to reach the basement and bathroom." In his book, Frankie recounted receiving a dime from the manager, Mr. Robertson, every Saturday morning. "A dime then would buy, splendidly, thirty jawbreaker candies. Six cents would buy a cola, but we would not waste money on something as transitory or fizzy as a soft drink. We could suck on jawbreaker, with multi-col- oured layers, for an age."

Once children were dropped off, their parents couldn't visit them for a month, after which one hour on Saturday afternoons was allowed. To break the bond between the parent and child, visits away from the home were forbidden. There was a row of lockers next to the concrete playroom for the children to store their outerwear. In the room was a wooden table, which they would fight to stand on top of. "This might have been to prepare us for life in the big boys' dorm, if only to dispel any idea that we could easily get rid of the boss boy," said Frankie. The bathroom cubicles didn't have doors, and there was one big bathtub where two boys would bathe at the same time. After bath time, the boys were inspected to be sure everyone was clean. Bedtime was always at seven p.m., and they slept in metal cots with wool army blankets, which protected them from the cold temperatures in the sunroom.

"We were stubbornly happy, defiant and mad about play. It would be no falsehood to say that we were a band of little, happy brothers," wrote Frankie. "Then, we were somewhat sheltered and were not yet aware that we would eventually go up to the big boy's dorm." The boys performed weekly chores. Some children left the home to attend a high school in Calgary, but others took classes at the home. There were church services a few times a week, during which they would sing psalms. After church, they went to a playground near the home.

At Christmas, local civic groups put on parties for the children. There would be a decorated tree and presents for everyone, from board games to candy. "Bread had immense value, as it was a kind of currency in the home then," said Frankie. "The statement 'You owe me two slices, chum,' was a regular expression." There were no snacks. They had eggs only twice a year, at Easter and Christmas. If a boy left due to an illness or injury, he almost never returned to the home. Children were always coming and leaving. After you graduated from grade nine, you left forever.

Once Frankie turned eight, he moved into the lower boys' room. By way of initiation, other boys urinated on his face. "I remember burying my face in the sink and flooding my mouth with icy water," he said. "I remember too a burning rage. I do not remember crying, though I have the Irish in me and tears come easy." Fights at the time were uncommon, although on one occasion the "boss boy" punched Frankie repeatedly in the face, and he remembers seeing older boys drag a child from the Scout house into the woods, where they tied him to a tree and whipped him with a homemade cat-o'-nine-tails. Younger boys who wet the bed would be forced run "the gauntlet" — a makeshift obstacle of swinging pillows. And a boy could expect retribution if he did anything that got the others in trouble. The supervisor had a private suite near the stairs, near which the strappings took place; every Alberta school teacher, at the time, had their own certified strap.

The big dorm had a bigger dining room, where girls sat on the right and boys on the left. Breakfast was porridge, toast and syrup; during winter, the children were fed a cup of milk and a spoonful of cod-liver oil. Chores included peeling potatoes, turnips, carrots and onions for their supper, which typically consisted of vegetables, shepherd's pie and Jell-O for dessert.

In 1950, Wood's built a new school building with separate rooms and a gymnasium. Frankie left the school for a couple of years to live with his father before returning in 1952, with some new clothes and a toy fire truck. When someone stole the toy, the boss boy told Frankie that he had to punch the offender, who turned out to be a dear friend. Frankie beat his face until it bled, and never fought again.

This is when Billy and his siblings arrived and started in the younger dorm. Billy would go on to learn the unwritten rules, which the older boys knew and enforced. "We were princes," said Frankie. "Billy and his buddies would be running around doing chores for us." Billy was lucky to arrive after the opening of the new school, which had a number of influential teachers who had no idea what was going on at the home. "I had learned to survive in that kind of *Lord of the Flies* world," said Frankie. One of the ways the boys stayed busy was by making weapons, such as slingshots and crossbows. Slingshot fights would break out in the summer. Violence wasn't constant, however, and the normal parts of childhood played out.

There was a polio epidemic in Canada at the time, and Billy spent his first summer at the home under quarantine with everyone else. The iron gates to the property were locked. Around the property were forests, prairies and the Bow River. "I could smell adventure, when rambling up on the expanses above the home site, on the wind, wafting from the front ranges of the mountain," wrote Frankie. "That must explain why I have always felt a pull to the west — have loved mountains. Wood's was a caged island on the edge of the north world within distance of the Rockies."

There were owls at night and bears that would wander by. Wildflowers bloomed on the slopes in the spring. Old-growth fir trees stood near the home; the students named one of them Three Sisters and tied branches together to use as a swing. The forest trails became a sanctuary for Billy and everyone else. A new supervisor, who Frankie remembers as "Mr. T.," arrived and pushed for more sports and outdoor time. In winter, the young boys played hockey on a small rink by the river. Fires would crackle in steel drums as the supervisors cheered loudly. For basketball uniforms, they used hockey jerseys and bathing suits. There was also weekly gymnastics training. Mr. T tried to give the boys more support than previous supervisors had, even getting them birthday cakes. However, he was also very heavy-handed when it came to discipline.

It was the next supervisor the home hired that made the most lasting impression on Billy. His name was Art Jeal. He was married and had a baby boy and a dog. Art introduced outdoor recreation such as camping, hiking and paddling. He even taught some backcountry navigation and survival skills. He encouraged the boys to keep track of their adventures in journals. During Frankie's early years, the boys would go to Kamp Kiwanis on the Elbow River for summer activities. But when Billy started, they began to visit Camp Chief Hector, north of the Bow River and beneath Mount Yamnuska. The peak, officially named Mount John Laurie, derives its common name from the Stoney Nakoda word *Îyâmnathka*, which translates to "flat-faced mountain."

Frankie left after finishing grade nine. He opted out of being put with a foster family and, with no money, he left for northern BC to be with his father. "I walked out through those old cast-iron gates and past the empty playground." Frankie wrote. "I never looked back as I strode out, so happy and optimistic. If I had, I would have seen that the Wood's experience trailed behind me." Frankie would go on to serve in the Royal Canadian Air Force, live in New Zealand and settle with his family in Kamloops, BC. He proudly wears a ring that says "Dad."

As Billy entered his teenage years, Wood's built cottages to replace the old dorms. It was going through a period of soul-searching to rid itself of the barracks reputation. However, at the same time, a man named William Engelke started as a supervisor. Frankie describes him as a British man who claimed he had fought as a commando against the Germans in North Africa, and who would go on to take advantage of his position and sexually assault many of the boys. "The truth," Frankie said, "is that he was a sadist and a rapist and a monster." William had a half-brother named Simpson, who he brought into his circle; Frankie says they would jointly assault boys. "That kind of predator was cruel to everyone," said Frankie, "but he would target the most vulnerable."

William would eventually go to court, where boys from the home testified against him. One of them was Billy. He would have been a witness and likely a victim, at least of attempts by William to have physical contact with him. The same can be said for Billy's brother, Ken. At the time, there was no charge in Alberta for pedophilia with boys 12 to 14 years old. William was charged in 1962 on three counts of gross indecency, a law designed to prosecute gay men. The primary victim was considered too young to appear in court. William was sentenced to just one year in the Lethbridge penitentiary.

Billy stayed at Wood's until 1964. When he left, he was placed in the home of a Mr. and Mrs. Walker, where he lived while he finished high school. His father still lived in Calgary, as did his sisters, but Billy didn't see them very often. He did spend time with his brother and some friends he'd made at Wood's.

"Billy would seem to exhibit to me — I'm no psychologist but I've read widely — quite a few of the symptoms of child abandonment, because I was [abandoned]," said Frankie. "Particularly the loss of or no maternal affection, or being deprived from your mother leaving, divorcing or being killed. Principal symptoms are alienation from society — I have felt that — and a mistrust of authority and people generally. It's hard to imagine people like that being able to build a connection with anybody, and in my case [with] other males. I had to learn how to outwit other boys at Wood's. What little I know about Billy's life, I read signs of profound alienation. Of course, there are many other factors, so we can't diagnose from a distance."

It was in 1960, during one of the summer trips to Camp Chief Hector, that Billy climbed his first mountain. It would change his life.

Chapter 3

ROCK CLIMBING

At length the Rocky Mountains came in sight like shining white clouds on the horizon, but we doubted what our guide said; but as we proceeded, they rose in height, their immense masses of snow appeared above the clouds, and formed an impassable barrier, even to the Eagle.

—*DAVID THOMPSON*

BILLY WAS 12 AND STILL LIVING AT WOOD'S Christian Home when he started a climbing journal. He narrated his adventures, added photos of mountains and talked about his friends. He used a pencil to write the journals on lined paper before typing them with a typewriter. His first entry was written in the Chief Hector cabin. The building had vertical log walls and a large caribou skull above the west-facing front porch. Billy and the other campers would sit outside around a campfire and watch Yamnuska fade into the evening. He wrote:

> We had been in camp about a week when we heard of our first climb. It was a mountain overlooking us, to the north-west. It was called Yamnuska, a Native name meaning wall of rock.

The next day, carrying packs which felt like a ton to me, we hiked to the base of the east ridge. Here we camped for one night and then began our climb of the "wall of rock." It was beautiful that day and my heart began to pound as we approached the huge mass of rock. It was not a difficult climb by any means. We just followed the ridge up. It was a hike, more or less.

When we got to the top, I was transfixed. The great height seemed to have me spellbound. Right from then I knew I would be doing more climbing.

We ate a small lunch, consisting of oranges and mountain mix which is a mixture of oatmeal, raisons, cocoa and sugar. Then we started down the back. Here I got my first experience at screeing. Scree is the rough rock or shale near the base of the mountain. Using an ice axe as a rudder we slid down it. When we reached the bottom, my running shoes, Scarpe da Gatto, were nearly torn off my feet. We had a short rest, then a long hike back to camp.

Things I learned: never throw rocks off of a mountain, due to might-be-present climbers, and how to avoid pine tree needles after your running shoes have been torn off while screeing. I've decided to keep a journal of my adventures.

Billy's second climb was on Easter weekend in 1964. He was staying at the Eisenhower Youth Hostels at the base of Castle Mountain in Banff National Park. The most commonly climbed rock route on Castle was up the east face of a peak called Eisenhower Tower. The climb wasn't overly demanding but covered a lot of vertical terrain. Along with Billy were some other campers and their supervisor, Mr. Thomas. Billy described him as "short, but a well-built athlete." It was the second-last day of the trip, and they were returning from a small hike to a waterfall. Billy wrote about how beautiful it was as they hiked down to the cabins.

Later that evening, they were sitting by the Johnson Canyon road between Eisenhower forest ranger station and the youth hostels when a car came speeding up with one occupant on board, the woman driving. She jumped out and ran for the ranger's house. Her friends were missing on the mountain. A guide from the Calgary Alpine Club who was on hand said he would go up to see if he could find them. Mr. Thomas volunteered himself and Billy to help. They packed boiled eggs, oranges and bread and started off. Billy said it was the fastest pace he'd ever ran. It normally took about two hours to get to the base, but they did it in about 45 minutes. At the cliff, they stopped to call the Banff ranger station by walkie-talkie. Billy wrote that "every time the guide went to talk, he pushed the listen button instead of the talk button. I told him this, which made me feel pretty good." So Mr. Thomas said, "Here, you take it." That was Billy's job from then on. They started up the first step, but it was getting dark and they had to sleep on the mountain. As soon as the full moon was high enough, they climbed by its light. The climb was Billy's *belle premiere*," as he wrote. He was scared to death half the time, and the rest, he was spellbound by the beautiful colours. He stood on the top of Eisenhower Tower, which they climbed without rope or protection. Most modern-day alpine climbers take at least one rope and plenty of equipment.

You can't imagine what the valley looked like from 3000 metres with a full moon and stars shining. It was beyond description. I do not know what time I reached the summit, but I do know that I was cold and hungry. So, we stopped and rested, had some rum and hard-boiled eggs, what a combination. The rum sure warms one up and I felt much better. All the time we were yelling at the top of our lungs the names of the people we thought were trapped up there. However, we found out later by walkie-talkie that they were down alright. Another thing which made our climb more rough was the fact that when I stopped to rest, a pack rat ate through the straps on the walkie-talkie. I had to carry the thing in my hands. Anyway, we finally got down to a warm bed and good food. Thanks to that guide, I forgot his name, for a most rewarding climb.

*   *   *

That winter, Billy was an honour roll student in high school and developed a fascination with mechanical objects. He had to find out how things worked, either by taking them apart or by building them. He even won at a local science fair with a robot he built that could crush a pop bottle. In the spring, he offered to take his 16-year-old friend Bruce Millis up a mountain. Billy chose Big Sister, a peak above Canmore. The Big Sister stood at 2936 metres and was no easy feat. It was first climbed in 1887, but the angle of the rock presented challenges that had turned away many would-be summiteers.

It was my first leading trip. It is something to tag-
along on a climb, but it is much more to lead one.
Here you have the responsibility of the group you
are leading and this doubles your enjoyment once on
top. You pick your own route up and it is you everyone looks up to for a safe climb.

They left Calgary and took the Greyhound to
Canmore, and from there made the long, hard trip up
the Spray Lakes Road on foot with big packs. A lumber
truck soon picked them up and dropped them off at
the base of the mountain, and they went for a swim in
the lake.

Their plan for the day was to make a raft from driftwood and bring firewood to camp. After ten hours of
collecting logs, they finished what Billy thought was
the best raft on the lake. They made several trips on
it, collecting driftwood for the fire, then made supper
and turned in. They were up early the next morning
and went out on the raft just for fun. Billy's "heart beat
madly" in anticipation of the climb. They took a small
pack with water, oranges and sandwiches. Billy was surprised at how deceptively challenging a mountain can
be. Near noon, Billy could see Bruce was tired, and they
stopped for lunch. The ridge was narrowing, with large
drops on either side. Finally they reached a spot where
Bruce, his own heart racing, said, "No sir, Billy, you go
on, but I'll just wait."

Bruce sat down and rested, and Billy looked for a
place to get around a notch in the ridge. The only way
was to jump to the other side, "grab the edge and then by
reestablishment, gain the upper ridge. Reestablishment
is pulling oneself up by arms alone." Billy asked Bruce

if he wanted to try. Bruce said no, but said to go ahead while he waited. Billy made it, and from there it was an easy hike to the top. Two ravens kept him company. Once on top, he snapped the remaining two pictures on his camera and had something to eat. He had brought up an old bean can, which he carved his name and date into before leaving it at the summit.

I slammed on the brakes and stopped about two feet from a sheer drop of about 600 metres. I just sat down there and tried to get my heart out of my throat. Finally, it came to me that Bruce was yelling, trying to find out what happened. I yelled back and said that everything was alright and that I would be back in a few minutes. When I got to him, I told him what had almost happened and then we started down the scree on the west side of the spine. It was a little steep, but not too bad and we were down in the gully in about 10 minutes. From there we slid on our butts the rest of the way to the woods. When we got back to camp, my whole back part of my pants was gone and so was the back of my underwear, boy was I air-conditioned. We had a well-earned meal and turned in very early. We stayed another three days just lazing around then we headed home. Thanks to Bruce Millis for a most enjoyable climb, he was very good on that climb.

*   *   *

In Canada's centennial year of 1967, when Billy turned 19, his friend John Braun invited him to go climbing.

It was early spring, and there was still a lot of snow in the mountains. A good climber, John had climbed Mount Temple's north face with George Senner, who had made the first ascent of Alaska's remote Mount Kennedy. Billy and John got a ride to Canmore with Mr. and Mrs. Walker, Billy's house parents, and started the long walk up the Spray Lakes Road. They made their way to a small lake and soaked their feet in the cold water. A strong wind was coming through the col above as they chatted about how nice the climbing looked on "Chinaman's Peak" (now Ha Ling Peak, named in honour of the first man to climb it, back in 1896).

They put their tent up and filled water bottles from a small stream. "The next day it was frozen and dried up, what a combination." After supper, they approached their planned route. Dark cloud from the west brought a bone-chilling wind. They came across a big snow slope and climbed it. They both had ice tools, but only John had crampons.

It was getting late so we glissaded down to base camp. This was our first attempt at glissading and what fun it was. Glissading: the art of skiing down on a glacier, on one's shoes, using an ice axe as a rudder. When we got to camp, we were frozen and wet and made a big fire to dry out. After having a couple of cups of hot tea, we retired to the tent: one-quarter of a parachute, light silk and waterproof, very light, but not good for high altitude climbing or bivouacking.

At 3 a.m. we started off. We roped up at 4:30 and started climbing the face. I was scared, but had faith in John. After reaching the first step we came upon a huge glacier. We had been climbing for eight hours. The wind was so bad that we put our coats and gloves back on. We were also very tired and thirsty and more than once I reached down for a handful of snow to suck on. We were soon back on rock and off the snow. The wind worsened, so we hunched over to climb. Once John got ahead of me, he sped up. When I looked up, I still could not see him. However, after a little climbing, I found him sleeping behind a big rock. Instead of waking him, I went over to the edge and took some pictures. John woke up and we continued on. John gave me an oxo-cube to suck on. Oh, was it awful, but I was hungry so I ate it anyway. Finally, we got to the top and what a view folded out before us.

We sat down and ate our one big orange before glissading until the snow softened, then just rolled or fell through as best as we could. After 10 hours on the mountain, our energy was drained. The snow was up to our belly buttons. Finally reaching the lower cliff, we climbed down without a rope. Too tired to do any acrobatics, we stumbled down. Back at camp, we collapsed into the tent and slept for a couple of hours. It was time for cold beans and cookies, then packing. We got a ride all the way back to Calgary on Monday morning.

The route Billy and John climbed was new, but they never officially recorded it. Billy drew a picture of Ha Ling Peak with a faint line where they climbed. It would be a decade before another new route was climbed up the face.

* * *

In June 1967, shortly after graduation, Billy and his old friend John Bruinink hitchhiked to Yamnuska to camp and attempt a climb.

> It seems funny when you are trying to get a ride, no large cars or trucks will pick you up. It is just small sport cars with hardly any room in them at all that give you rides. This is how we got our ride, in a small red sport car. What a crowded ride we had in that little can, but thanks to those two lads for giving us a ride... I had a good night's sleep and we got up at about three thirty in the morning. It was still overcast, the clouds being even lower, but it was not raining. After a breakfast of grapefruit, water and rye bread, we packed a small knap-sack with oranges and a few squished sandwiches and started up the base.

They had a 150-foot rope, pitons, slings and several carabiners. Soon after climbing they were right in the clouds themselves. They could not see the mountain, nor the valley below, just clouds all around them.

> It sure gave me a strange feeling to be climbing steeply up and not see our starting point. The climb was a very hard one. My opinion, and many would agree with it, is that scree climbing is the hardest part of any climb. That long steep hill of grass and stones, just before the mountain, can really tire one out.

As they hiked along the base, making sure not to slip down into the clouds below, Billy noticed name plates attached to the rock. They identified the different routes up the face, including Unnamed, King's Chimney and Direttissima. In total there were 13.

John and Billy reached the route they had planned to climb and started to rope up. Billy had a "good smoke." John was going to lead, so Billy got ready to belay. It was raining a little harder, but they went on. The first part of the climb consisted of a chimney some 60 feet in height. At the top of this there was a small platform, a good place to belay from. John went up first and Billy let out the rope as he did so.

> A chimney is nothing but a large crack in the rock face with a fairly large opening on the outside. To climb it, you sort of jam yourself into it and work your way up. There is no really stated way to do it, because the chimney varies in so many ways. We put our feet on one wall, and our back against the other wall; then by putting force against both walls, we just sort of shimmied up. The main trouble with a lot of new climbers is the tendency to force oneself into the chimney too far. The main reason why most people do this is because of the exposure. What one should do is to stay out as much as possible and not jam oneself too far into the crack. What happens is the climber is so pushed in that he loses his grip and probably falls.

John took about 15 minutes to climb it (he and John Braun had done it once before). Then he got to a ledge and was going to belay Billy. However, Billy was wearing a pack containing their lunch, which made it hard to go up the chimney. So he tied the pack to the rope and then John just pulled it up. As he did so, Billy let out the rope from below, making sure that the pack did not get stuck on the way.

After this maneuver, I went up. I was scared, but really enjoyed myself. I made it, to John's surprise, in about 10 minutes. We worked up a little further and then to my surprise John said, "Here Billy, you lead."

It was still raining as John gave me all the hardware for leading. Below us, we could see the cliff dropping into the grayness below; what an eerie view. The climb was really easy until we got about ¾ way. Here I reached a very difficult chimney which involved a very hard maneuver. In order to get to the second platform, I had to drive a piton into the crack above me. I was doing this up about 2,000 feet. With one foot in a sling and the other one jammed into the crack I supported himself by hanging on to a piton that he had driven into a crack just below the over-hang. I also had a biner and rope through a piton for safety's sake. After about an hour of sweating in the rain, I managed to make this part; I let out a yell of happiness just from the relief. I had been so scared that my mouth was dry and my throat sore. I was shaking very badly, so I sat down to let my body relax.

I drove in another piton and belayed John up. It took him about 15 minutes to come up the rope and pull out all the work I had just put in. When he got to the platform he told me that the last piton I had used, the one I had all my weight on, was so loose that he pulled it out with his fingers. My heart went right up into my throat and then I really needed a ciga-rette. We decided to rest for a little while so I lit up a well-deserved smoke. Looking down, all I could see was clouds, rain and more rain. Here we also found a log to sign. It was a small tin can, water-proof and fastened to a piton, and so we signed it. My com-ments were, "Scary as hell, but a nice climb." John's comment was, "Interesting." John told me about the time John Braun, Klaus Berger and he did the route in winter. He had nearly fallen off that spot while trying to do it with snow and ice all over the rock.

After a 15-minute rest, I led the climb to the top. There was no rain or cold on the far side of the mountain. You see, the mountain acted as a barrier to the storm and therefore had held the clouds out of the valley. It was sunny and beautiful and this in itself gave me a great lift. I felt tremendous and all the hardships of the climb seemed to disappear. However, as I was belaying John, clouds suddenly closed in all around us. By the time we got to the summit it was raining. We were afraid of lightning so we retreated down the back to a lower point.

The Unnamed Route Billy and John had climbed is, by today's standards, a moderate rock climb. They climbed in their leather boots, did not wear helmets or harnesses and did not have modern safety gear. Billy called it "the best rock climb of my entire life," but noted he was "very mad about not getting more pic-tures, but the rain and lack of light was too much for my little Brownie Star-Flash."

*   *   *

Billy then teamed up again with John Braun for another climb on Yamnuska that would turn out to be Billy's first defeat — largely due to the fact that they started up the wrong climb.

> We started up the long, steep hill. The bugs were bad, but the day looked good. There were a few rain showers, but this we found a relief from the rising temperatures. When we reached the base, we stopped to arrange equipment at the bottom of Grillmair Chimneys. We hadn't intended on climbing anything that day and only brought a small utility rope. Not long after starting, we found a hole in the top of the mountain, which provided the only access to the top. John said he would lead the first pitch, then I could lead to about ¾ way. It was fun and games from then on because we could not find the route. We just went up and it turned out to be a really hard climb. The Grillmair Route is supposed to be quite easy, but we were finding it the opposite. Later, we realized we were climbing to the east of the route. Anyway, up we went.
>
> We reached a small cave under a large overhang. I crawled into this and came out into a huge cavern. It was cold in there, but I was too spell-bound to notice. It was gigantic. We went up the steep wall and came out over the overhang, "just like the Matterhorn in the Alps," John said. John took over because we had arrived at a real hard pitch. We used every piton, sling and biner we had, but were unable to make the

summit. We tried for hours, but still came out beaten. I remember standing there, belaying John, watching him cursing and struggling on the smooth face. At one point, he nearly fell because he was getting tired of holding onto nothing. After much fighting on that ---- mountain, we gave up and rappelled down, leaving some of our equipment on the face. We had to in order to rappel. We were going to get John Bruinink to show us the right route because he had done it before.

It was hard to rappel down because we were tired and discouraged from our defeat. We tried to leave as few pitons up as possible. A lot of times we used rocks as a rappel base. I was scared most of the time.

*   *   *

That same summer, mere weeks after his triumph with Billy on Yamnuska, Bruinink fell to his death while soloing on Mount McGillivray, a peak about 90 kilometres west of Calgary, one of the mountains that had become newly accessible with the 1962 opening of the Trans-Canada Highway. The report in *American Alpine Journal Accidents* read:

Alberta, Rockies, Mt. McGillivray. On 8 July John Bruinink (19) left Calgary and hitch hiked into Rockies to make a scrambling course. He had previously laid out the trail three weeks before. He said he "may go climbing." He was supposed to have had a rope although none was found near the body.

On 10 July search party located the body, climbing hardware, hammer, rucksack and water bottle. Body was found two to three miles southwest of where he was supposed to be going and there were no signs of his having been in the intended location. His wrist watch was stopped at 3:15-3:20, presumably p.m. He apparently fell while climbing alone.

Billy was on holiday with his father when the news reached him. He returned home only to find that he had missed the funeral by a day. Billy hadn't seen John since they were on Yamnuska. He remembered huffing and puffing up the steep hill while John ran the rest of the way.

I know John died at what he loved to do. He loved the adventure, the danger, the beauty of the wilderness as well as the just plain climbing. From here on, John Braun and I will promise to put a plaque on the mountain that took his life.

Billy and John packed their climbing equipment and a plaque that read: "In memory of John Bruinink, 1947-1967, W.L. Davidson, J.E. Braun." They left one Friday night after school and got a ride from Billy's brother, Ken, out to the base of McGillivray. They hiked to the top of the rock wall on Saturday morning and left the plaque sitting in a pile of rocks overlooking the valley.

A few weeks later, they returned to Yamnuska to climb another route. John hitchhiked out with his sister before Billy, who was finally picked up by a truck driver.

Commenting on how hard hitchhiking was getting, Billy blamed "those damn tourists." At the base of Yamnuska, they found the start of King's Chimney.

John was leading and as he worked to get a belay piton in, he smashed his thumb. He could not move it, so I was sure that he had broken it. I worked my way up to him without belay protection and fixed him to the rock wall so as to give him some protection. We decided that since we were so close to the summit we would try for it. I started up, inching my way up the over-hanging wall. It was hard going and I was scared to death. I would never have done it, but John was in very bad trouble.

I was up about 100 feet when I nearly fell. The ground was some 800 feet below where I was hanging on vertical rock. I'd used all my "spoons" (very flat pitons) and was going up without any close support. After about five feet, the verticalness changed into an overhang. This is where I fell. I cannot explain how I felt because it happened so fast. John later said that he heard me yell and thought I had reached the summit, a victory yell. He then said he heard scraping sounds. By some luck, I was able to stay close to the wall as I fell. Doing so, I was frantically grabbing for support. I finally managed to stop before gaining too much momentum. Through all this I fell only about 10 feet. I stood on a very small ledge, hands bleeding and legs shaking. Then I was able to hear John and yelled back. Hanging on with one hand, I managed to get a smoke into my mouth. I drew the smoke deeply into my lungs. This helped to calm me down. I'm not trying to sell them either, the smokes really helped. I yelled to John to find out how his thumb was. He replied with some hesitation, "Alright."

Of course, I knew he was lying and that he was really in a lot of pain. I then started to look for another way up, but was stopped when John yelled, "Let's get off this fucking mountain." So, I drove in a piton and rappelled down to where he sat in pain. He sure had a lot of guts, as soon as I got down, he began to drive in a piton to rappel down the rest of the way. This he did as he moaned from pain. Bad luck was still playing tricks on us. When I went to pull the rope down, it wouldn't come down. The — thing was stuck up at the belay spot. So, I had to climb up and get it going straight again. I was still very shaken up, but I had to do it in order to get down.

*　　*　　*

A week after King's Chimney, Billy was looking forward to another outing in the mountains. He looked up an old friend from school. At 19, Pat Holt had no real climbing experience, but Billy was sure that he could follow behind an easy route. They headed for Yamnuska. Ken gave them a ride up to the old base camp just below the mountain. They got to the base of the route at 11 a.m., and Billy led up in hot weather. He could see that Holt was having fun. The climb lasted about six hours. "Thanks to Pat Holt for a most rewarding climb," Billy wrote.

He then teamed up with Paul Nelson to attempt a climb on Goat Mountain, west of Yamnuska, called the Ramp. It followed a long section of slabby rock to a short wall, followed by easier climbing. It had been climbed only once, in 1961.

It was really beautiful out and already my heart began to feel like it was going to burst, it was pounding so hard. We got ready to climb with myself leading the whole way, the climbing was fun with the hardest pitch being about the third. We reached the secondary summit (Gendarme) at about noon. We had a rest, made a cairn and had something to eat. All of a sudden, we heard thunder coming down the valley from Banff, a rain storm was moving like a speeding train. Paul became worried about it, but I told him that it would pass right by. It did, but Paul wanted to get off the top, so unhappily I led the way down the back.

We went around the north side of the mountain and then back up to the pass between Goat Mountain and Yamnuska. From here I took my last look at the summit I came so close to having, then headed for camp. It is something which is hard to explain, but you really feel bad not reaching something when it is so near at hand. It is even worse when you have fought so hard for it and could have got it, if it weren't for some little thing. I could have gone alone, but climbing alone is a little dangerous.

*   *   *

Billy's 12th rock climb was back up on Yamnuska. He and John Braun climbed a new route at the east end of the mountain, where the cliffs were shorter than up the middle of the wall. It was called Raven's End after the many ravens that soared and nested on and around it. The climbs weren't long, but the rock was steep and the climbing challenging. Billy and John found an easy path through some big roofs east of a climb called Gollum Grooves. It was a first ascent, but they never recorded their new route in any guidebook.

The purpose of the climb was to make a movie on climbing in the Canadian Rockies. We planned to make it in two parts, summer and winter climbing. John's father was game and we were glad because he owned the film shop in Calgary's Bowness. This meant that he could be the camera-man and could use the real expensive movie cameras with a zoom-lens. I gave 10 dollars for film and John and his father helped with the rest.

We shot 45 dollars' worth of colour and sound tracks, super-8 movie film. We had about 28 minutes showing how one gets to the mountain, base camp, rock climbing, rope tying and rappelling. The climb we did took about one hour and we had fun most of the time. I must commend John's father on getting up that hill and for getting up the mountain, part-way. He is not the youngest man in the world and therefore did very well in getting up and filming the climb. Anyway, the climb was quite easy. It is recorded on film and therefore not worth recording in the log.

At the start of September 1967, John, his sister and Billy travelled to the Okanagan Valley in BC to climb cliffs near Penticton. It was Billy's first trip to BC. They drank beer by a lake and climbed a small rock wall. Once on top of the rock, they rappelled back down using a tree as an anchor. They climbed, swam, waterskied and partied. Billy fell in love with the relaxed BC life. "It was breathtaking," he wrote about the Okanagan Valley. On their way home, they stopped at Lake Louise, and John showed Billy the Tower of Babel, a quartzite peak that he had climbed that summer.

After the first two weeks of school, with the exception of playing football, Billy was fed up with city life. He gave John a call to see if he wanted to go on a climb. They planned on attempting King's Chimney again. Billy arrived at the camp first and lit a small fire. He rolled some cigarettes and waited for John.

> The sky was dark and clear. It was a little chilly, but nice. The stars were out in full-force, as I let the fire burn down. I did not know how long John would be, so I crawled into his sleeping bag and waited. A few minutes later, or so I thought, I awoke to see something shining brightly outside. I found it to be the moon out in full brilliance. I must have slept for quite a while, for some three hours had passed. I thought of making a fire, but decided to save the firewood I had worked so hard to collect. John had not arrived yet, so I was getting a little worried. He probably got out on the highway too late and therefore was

unable to get a ride. He would probably get in in the morning.

I went over into a clearing to have a look at the beautiful view. I really felt alone, but the view took all worries away. The full moon was lighting up the whole countryside, as if it were day. Yamnuska was all lit up and shining in the moonlight. It looked all pink and unreal. It stood out against the dark, star-filled sky, as if it were some sort of ghost. All the mountains to the west were shining brightly also and looked so close. As I stood there, a falling star shot behind Yamnuska.

While Billy was marvelling at the view, he heard a yell followed by boots on gravel. John had finally arrived — he'd had trouble getting a ride and had been dropped off a long hike away from the base camp. But there was still time for sleep before the morning's climb.

As the sun rose, we did too. We got breakfast going and got our equipment sorted out for the climb. We had just finished breakfast when a car came into the parking lot, near the camp. It turned out to be climbers, who after a little questioning, we found out to be a couple of good ones. They were planning to do the Direttissima route on Yamnuska. This was a real hard climb and I was hoping to see them doing it.

After signing the climber's log, we got under way. They were just up ahead of us and I think they were trying to keep ahead. They would see us coming and then quickly they would go faster. I thought it was quite humorous. We did an almost record time up that hill and were at the base of the mountain by about seven o'clock. It was a nice day and we got to their route in good time. As we went below the Direttissima, we could see the other climbers up at the rock base, getting set to do the route.

I got up to the gate, a well-known part of the Unnamed Route. I then led the traverse over to the beginning of the King's Chimney and another two pitches and then John took over. We went up the main chimney and did not miss the second traverse to the left. Last time, we missed this and ended up higher on an almost vertical face. We had this time studied the climber's logbook and would not make the same mistake.

A light wind was coming up which made the climb even more enjoyable. Everything seemed to be going so well that I felt something bad must happen. However, throughout the whole climb, we had a perfect trip. About halfway up, John and I found a platform to stop and have lunch on. It was hot, so I took my shirt off and had lunch. What a way to eat.

After lunch, we got on our way. I changed into running shoes, which are better than climbing boots in some cases. It was going easy till we came to a small traverse, which angled down about 10 feet, then came the hard part. After the small traverses, I had to go up a pitch of 120 feet, which had next to nothing for handholds. Below me, the rock face dropped to the ground, a long way. After a little work, I finally made it. I belayed John up and then started on the last pitch.

It was quite easy and at last we stood on top. We had beaten a route which had only a little while ago beaten us. It was a conquest in its entirety. We really felt good as we took the remaining pictures. We then headed back down and as we went by the Direttissima, we could see tiny red specks on its massive rock face. Maybe one day I will be up there.

* * *

Billy went back to school and started to edit his climbing footage. That winter, he visited Premier Sports a number of times. He'd first been to the store earlier that year to buy new climbing boots. On that visit, he'd met climber Brian Greenwood of the Calgary Mountain Club (CMC), who was working at the climbing counter, and they talked for hours about Brian's climbs around the world. Billy had written in his journal that Brian "was a great guy and I hope to climb with him someday, maybe a new route." Brian had led the 1961 first ascent of the Ramp on Goat Mountain, which Billy had teamed up with Paul Nelson to climb.

In the spring of 1968, Billy went into the store to buy some carabiners. Brian wasn't there — he had travelled to Chamonix to complete a mountain guide course, leaving Calgary climber Chic Scott to run the climbing counter. After chatting with Billy about climbing, Chic invited Billy to the next meeting of the vaunted CMC. Less than a week later, Billy was a member.

Chapter 4

CALGARY MOUNTAIN CLUB

*The Calgary Mountain Club was pretty much the Hells
Angels of the mountaineering world at the time.*
—BRUCE KELLER

*The club is a biker gang. Once you're a member you can
never not become a member.*
—URS KALLEN

A drinking club with a climbing problem.
—CHIC SCOTT

THE FIRST MEETING OF THE CALGARY
Mountain Club was held on June 8, 1960 by a group
of new Canadian climbers, mostly from Britain, New
Zealand, Germany and Austria. Other mountain clubs
at the time were focused on tradition. The CMC was
different. Here, climbers could plan cutting-edge adventures and party. The club fell very much in line with
what Jack Kerouac had prophesied in his 1958 novel
The Dharma Bums:

> I see a vision of a great rucksack revolution
> thousands or even millions of young Americans

wandering around with rucksacks, going up to mountains to pray, making children laugh and old men glad, making young girls happy and old girls happier, all of 'em Zen Lunatics who go about writing poems that happen to appear in their heads for no reason and also by being kind and also by strange unexpected acts keep giving visions of eternal freedom to everybody and to all living creatures.

In the wake of the Second World War, European and British immigrants brought innovative climbing techniques that laid the groundwork for the golden age of Canadian climbing. Canada already had a strong heritage of German and Austrian climbers and skiers; the new influx of British climbers brought updated technical skills to the Rockies. Those techniques became the foundation of the CMC.

One of those newcomers was Brian Greenwood, a clean-shaven, big-eared 21-year-old who moved from England to Calgary in 1956 and became one of Alberta's best rock and ice climbers. In *Pushing the Limits*, Chic Scott quotes Brian's account of his arrival:

> The first weekend in Calgary I caught the Greyhound bus out to Banff. I had my rucksack and my tent and I went up to the Alpine Club... I walked up there in the dark and I was scared of bears jumping out... I got to the Alpine Club and I said, "Can I stay here?" "No. No. You can't stay here." So, I walked all the way back down, still scared of bears.

He slept behind the Natural History Museum, and the next day, he climbed Mount Rundle. Over the next few years, he went on to make the fourth ascent of the mighty Mount Alberta, the sixth-highest peak in the Rockies. The first climbers up Alberta were a group of Japanese Alpine Club members, in 1925. They left a silver ice axe on the summit, which was later brought down to a museum. Brian led what he thought was the first ascent of Grand Sentinel, only to find an old hemp sling on the summit. Nobody knows who first climbed the tall quartzite tower that stands in the shadow of Mount Temple.

Once the CMC was formed, Brian and famed artist Glen Boles made the first winter traverse of Mount Rundle. The 23-kilometre climb took them over steep rock and 11 summits, and through deep, corniced snow ridges. At night, the lights from Canmore illuminated the snowy slopes along the valley. Later that year, Brian, along with three other climbers, made the first ascent of the northeast face of Ha Ling Peak. They followed low-angled slabs to a small roof and a long corner system that looked like it had been cut out of the mountain with a knife. Brian had become Canada's leading rock climber.

Many of the routes at the time were climbed using aid techniques with pitons and carabiners. Climbers used hammers to drive pitons into cracks in the rock. The pitons were fixed until removed with a hammer. It allowed climbers to ascend difficult sections of rock using direct aid when needed. More frequently, pitons hammered into the rock were used to secure the belayer or as protection for free climbing.

Brian's attention was soon focused on Yamnuska, which became his and the CMC's stomping ground for the next 20 years. They risked their lives in the name of adventure to push difficult rock climbs up the most obvious lines.

The first ascent of Yamnuska's big wall was in 1952 by Hans Gmoser, Isabel Spreat and Leo Grillmair. They followed a big chimney near the middle of the face, using only a nylon rope, no carabiners or pitons. Isabel wore Vibram-soled boots, Leo wore crepe-soled shoes and Hans might have worn leather ski boots. It was a bold ascent that set the standard for the mountain.

When the CMC formed, it organized events like the Sunwapta Giant Slalom ski race on Parker Ridge on the Icefields Parkway south of Jasper, Alberta, and an annual film and lecture night with Hans Gmoser. Over the next few years, Hans would go on to establish the heli-ski industry. In 1964, in the three/four col above Moraine Lake in the Valley of the Ten Peaks, the CMC constructed a bivouac hut named after Graham Cooper, who was killed during construction. It provided shelter for climbers aiming for routes like the icy north faces of Mounts Fay and Quadra and was later replaced with the Neil Colgan hut.

Brian's first new route on Yamnuska was with Ron Thomson in 1957. He called it Belfry. It was a bold first route for any new Yamnuska climber. "The more you went up, the more you saw of it, the more you became attached to it," Brian said about Yamnuska. He added many routes up the most obvious climb-vertical paths before embarking on one of the most ambitious routes of the day: Red Shirt. He climbed the meandering route with Heinz Kahl and Dick Lofthouse.

The climbers of the CMC needed specialized equipment, but no store in Calgary supplied it. American climber Yvon Chouinard, who made a number of important first ascents in Canada, went on to become a well-known blacksmith for the pitons and carabiners that he made in a shed in California. On his trips to Canada, he'd fill the trunk of his car with climbing gear to sell to climbers north of the border. Brian started to import climbing gear from around the world and sell it out of his Elbow Park home — everything from Himasport down apparel and Galibier boots to Charlet ice tools and Chouinard's pitons. His house was where CMC climbers partied late into the night. His library was the most impressive of any club member's; books like *Conquistadors of the Useless* and *The White Spider* stirred the imaginations of the young Calgary climbers and inspired many future climbs.

In 1963, CMC members established the Mountain Rescue Committee, which became the Calgary Mountain Rescue Group. The group assisted with rescues on peaks outside the national park, mostly on Yamnuska. Brian went on to climb more serious routes on Yamnuska, ones where a fall could leave a climber dead. He had many partners over the years, climbers he'd trust his life to: Don Vockeroth, Lloyd MacKay, Dick Lofthouse and many others. Don, who opened many challenging routes, said, "Every time you climbed up to the base, we would sit down and just think about it. Think about the things that we did, think about where you were in the world and how great things in life were." While there were great successes on Yamnuska, the first fatality took place in 1964, when 18-year-old Brian Anderson fell and died trying to free-solo Unnamed Route. His friends found his body at the base of the climb.

In the mid-1960s, local teenagers joined the CMC, climbers like Don Gardner and Charlie Locke. Chic also joined during this time. The club was growing, and everyone was gaining more experience. There were a few Canadian climbers in the club, but most members were from abroad. The standard of local climbing was almost on par with what was going on in more populated climbing areas like Yosemite and Chamonix. Brian and Charlie put their skills to the test on the north face of Mount Temple. They climbed over a kilometre of stacked limestone, quartzite and bands of coal. The mountain was called the "Eiger of the Rockies," and their new route was cutting-edge. Although Brian claimed "it wasn't that hard," it went on to be a Canadian alpine test-piece.

It was then that Swiss climber Urs Kallen moved to Toronto with his wife, Gerda. Urs had done new climbs on Ontario rock faces like Bon Echo before moving west and settling in Calgary in the summer of 1966. "Yamnuska is so interesting," Urs told me. "It depends on the light that you see it in. All of a sudden you see lines that you only see in certain light." Urs's friend Klaus Hahn took him up to Yamnuska that year, and they made the first ascent of the Toe, a tower of tiered pinnacles that looks like a foot. The crumbly chimney to reach the biggest toe required them to press their feet against opposite walls, a skill called bridging. Ravens were a daily sighting on Yamnuska, and three circled Urs and Klaus as they rappelled down their climb.

The following year, Brian and Urs hiked up to the base of Yamnuska in hopes of climbing a new route. On the way up, they stopped at the new rescue hut, which had a fibreglass roof and stored gear for rescues.

Urs then spotted a line that they dubbed the Super Direct. Up at the base of Yamnuska, they slung pitons and hammers over their shoulders. Brian tightened his leather boots and buckled his helmet. In the autumn snow, Brian led the first pitch. It followed stacks of square limestone held together with mud to a left-trending feature. At the top of the pitch, Brian hammered two pitons into a snow-filled crack and rappelled back to Urs.

The heavy snows that winter created sloughing snow from the side of Yamnuska. The new rescue hut was struck by either an avalanche or rockfall and destroyed. The following summer, after the snow had melted, Brian and fellow British climber John Moss climbed what would become the hardest route on Yamnuska for the next decade. The route, named Balrog, took Brian many attempts over a number of years. It followed one of the most intimidating and overhanging chimneys on Yamnuska. No climber has ever ventured into the void the chimney leads to. Brian named it after a fictional creature in *The Lord of the Rings*. His passion for Tolkien's saga led him to name a number of routes, and even some of his children, after its characters.

It was around then that Brian started working at the climbing desk at a store called Premier Sports — where, in 1967, he met a young Billy Davidson looking for a new pair of boots.

Chapter 5

BUGABOO SPIRES

Hammocks tonight. Twilight is incredible. All around
jagged towers, ice and desolate valleys... leaving the
Howsers as they are this very day; eagles slowly circling
mist enshrouded towers.
—*HUGH BURTON*

IN THE SUMMER OF 1968, BILLY AND OTHER CMC
members approached a daunting new challenge:
the Bugaboos. Originally called the Nunataks, this
group of granite peaks in BC's Purcell Mountains was
renamed when an ill-fated gold rush ended below it
— "bugaboo" is prospecting slang for a dead end. The
first climb in the Bugaboos has become one of the
most famous in early Canadian climbing history. The
renowned Austrian guide Conrad Kain guided Albert
and Bess McCarthy and John Vincent up a long ridge on
Bugaboo Spire in 1916. The Bugaboos have a number of
summits, notably the Howser Towers, Pigeon, Bugaboo,
Snowpatch and Crescent.

CMC members made trips to the Bugaboos every
summer, when the weather was suitable: unlike limestone, granite can be hard to climb when wet or snowy,

so July and August were the preferred months. Visiting Calgarians drove west and then south to Radium Hot Springs before heading north towards Golden. Halfway between Radium and Golden, they drove west on logging roads to within a few hours' hike of the Bugaboo Glacier. They would pack their gear at the end of the rutted road with ancient ice rolling over granite walls visible in the distance. Grizzly bears wandered in the forests where the ice terminated into streams. More than once, climbers ran into hungry grizzlies on the hike in.

In 1964, Hans Gmoser started using helicopters to transport skiers into the remote Bugaboo Spires. Many climbers, including the legendary Fred Beckey, criticized the helicopter use, but Gmoser was so successful that in 1968 he built a high mountain lodge near the spires. Bugaboo Lodge was the base for skiers in the winter, but in the summer, it was a stopover spot for climbers.

In 1961, Fred Beckey and Yvon Chouinard made the first ascent of the west buttress of the South Howser Tower. The massive wall hadn't been seen by climbers until 1960, when Fred descended past ice falls and found it. Fred had already climbed in the Bugaboos, with Brian in 1959, when the two climbed a new ten-pitch route on Snowpatch Spire. Then, in 1963, they climbed together again when they made the first ascent of the east face of Oubliette in the Tonquin Valley near Jasper. They made plans to climb again the following year in the Bugaboos. They teamed up for the demanding route up the northwest buttress of the North Howser Tower, the first ever climb up that side of the mountain.

Fred and Brian were experts at climbing ice-covered and rotten rock, overhanging walls and drenched slabs. In the summer of 1968, Brian returned to the Bugaboos, but without Fred. Instead, he visited with CMC members. During that trip, he met Rob Wood, a top climber who'd just visited Yosemite, where he and Mick Burke had become the first all-British team to climb the Nose on El Capitan. Brian invited them back to his Calgary house once their trip to the Bugaboos was over for a "piss up," as Rob said. Fifty years later, Rob wrote in *Gripped* magazine:

> During the next few years I was lucky enough to rope up with Brian on several first ascents in the Rockies. I'm sure anyone who has ever been on a big route with Brian will agree what a privilege that was. He was undoubtedly the master at that time. His ability to remain calm and positive with his laconic and highly irreverent humour and the camaraderie it generated, even in extremely scary circumstances, was inspirational even transformational.

After an arduous first ascent of Kelloggs on Mount Kitchener in 1972, Brian, Rob and George Homer spent three days in a bar. Their bender ended in a brawl that left blood spattered on tables and walls. Brian and George spent a night in jail. Reflecting on the "culture shock" they'd experienced on returning to Banff, and the "reality we perceived as pretentious and super-ficial" — a perception that prompted the mayhem — Wood noted that this was a turning point in the climb-ers' lives: in its aftermath, they eased off on the extreme adventures and "searched and found lifestyles that took us back to the land, with small doses of adventure and connectivity with nature in our everyday lives."

The first Calgary Mountain Club climb in the Bugaboos in 1968 was up the south face of Crescent Towers, above the Boulder Camp, where the climbers had rigged their tents and built cooking pits. It was climbed by Brian, Ron Thomson, Urs, Oyvind Berle and Dick Lofthouse. This was the first ascent of the face, and they called it Ears Between. A few days later, Dick and Brian climbed another new route called Left Dihedral, a steep aid climb that required tricky rope pendulums. Hans Gmoser joined the CMC climbers, and they made the first ascent of Lion's Way. During the last week of July, Brian and Oyvind made the first one-day ascent of the east face of Bugaboo Spire and the first by a non-American team. At the time, this was the test-piece big wall in the Bugaboos. It rose above the Boulder Camp for hundreds of metres and ended on the pointy summit of Bugaboo Spire. It was first climbed by Ed Cooper, from Squamish, and Art Gran. To descend, climbers down-climbed and rappelled the Kain Route.

It was during that week that Billy and his friends arrived in the Bugaboos, his first visit. As Billy later wrote, their trip did not start well:

Barbara Budd, Ray Horgan, Jack Bolton and myself wedged our way into Ray's Ford. My apology to Jack for I forgot a very important member. Jack's dog, Rastus, was also along. Jack said that his dog loves long trips like this. Poor thing, he'll never forget this one.

We arrived at Radium around midnight. The only one who knew the way to the Bugaboos was Barb. That was our first bit of bad luck. We slowly drove north from Radium waiting for Barb to point out the turn-off. Four turn-offs later, we arrived at the one which Barb was sure led to the Bugaboos.

From here, we merely drove around in dusty circles. At one place the car bounced over a large rock. After that it began to act rather funny. The motor would be running fine, then our forward motion was decreasing by the minute. Finally, the car came to a halt, just as we reached the end of the road we were on. We decided to stay here and then have a look at the car in the morning.

I was awakened by something wet sliding over my face. It turned out to be Rastus's tongue. It made a hasty retreat as I got up.

What a strange world surrounded us. We had stopped in an area which was all plowed up. There must have been a big fire here at one time, because the whole area was studded with burnt remains of trees.

I heard a roar from down the road. It was an old logging truck. I said good morning as the driver stepped out, looking rather bewildered. I guess he thought I was the only one there. However, when Jack appeared from under a bit of canvas, Ray from under the car, Barb from inside the car and Rastus from I don't know where, he showed some signs of understanding to our situation.

While he told us how we had gone wrong, Ray was checking out the car. After finding out how far back the turn-off was, I began to feel a little better. However, Ray found out that his transmission was cracked and that he had lost all the fluid.

So, without breakfast, we began to hike back down the road to the fork, some five miles away. We carried all of our equipment because we planned to head for the Bugaboos. However, on arriving at the turn-off, hot and tired, we decided to stop and have breakfast.

Jack and I would hike into the Bugaboos, about another 20 miles, while Ray and Barb made their way back to Spillimacheen. There they would see about getting the car towed out, fixed and then hitchhike back to meet us that evening. We waved farewell as we hiked in our prospective direction. Finally, we rounded a curve and there they were. Granite spires jutting out of the Bugaboo Glacier.

Arriving at Boulder Camp, Billy and Jack found themselves again in the company of fellow climbers, and learned about Brian's current exploits on the Bugaboos.

There were a few people standing about pointing out further climbs and drinking wine. Mostly drinking. The mosquitoes were very bad, but my cigarette smoke helped to drive some of them away. Boulder Camp is one of the most memorable places I've been to. I cannot explain the feeling one gets while standing among great climbers in this fantastic place.

As evening drew on, Jack and I went about meeting other climbers to try to organize something tomorrow. We found out that Brian Greenwood and another fellow were doing the east face of Bugaboo Spire. They were attempting to do it in one day. As we stood around the fire, we could pick out the headlamps as they descended. Just then, Ray came staggering into camp with Barb far behind. He said that we would be hitchhiking home on Monday night because there was nothing open to repair the truck. Ray made himself and Barb some supper. Brian came jingling into camp after a very successful climb.

Despite his limited granite experience, Billy agreed to climb the Snowpatch Route on Snowpatch Spire, a classic first climbed in 1940 by Jack Arnold and Raffi Bedayn. It follows a line of cracks up the left side of the sweeping east face and bypasses the glacier for which it's named. Barb planned to join a different group climbing Pigeon Spire.

The sunrise on Snowpatch was beautiful as we got our hardware and ropes sorted out. After a small breakfast, we headed out. After boulders brought us onto the glacier, we traversed below the east side of Snowpatch. Then we climbed up to where the normal route began.

The granite was just great as we moved up the first inside corner. Ray led while Jack was middle man. I was on the end for photographs. After the inside corner, we reached the first difficult pitch. A short hand traversed followed by a short overhanging wall. I could have used R.V.s on that traverse. After that it was an easy climb up slabs beside the snow patch. About there the difficulty increases. A series of inside corners and chimney led to the first hard move. A tricky hand traverse then up to the ridge. However, Ray went off route here, as do many, I hear, because of a sling dangling out on the face.

Over there, Ray had to climb back down and over to where he had started. It was a very good move and made for a good photograph. Once over that you have made it.

As Jack belayed me up this last part, I heard a strange sound behind me. When I asked Ray about it, he and Jack said they'd heard it before. Apparently, it was a charge building up in my ice axe. Off came my pack. Down I went into a small cave with the others. It was raining slightly so we had lunch and waited for it to stop. Afterwards, we moved up to the southwest side to rappel. All the slings were in, which made for a quick descent. We hiked back around the west face and down the col between Snowpatch and Bugaboo Spire. We could see Brian's tracks just after the bergschrund. Ray was a little ahead when a huge block fell off the east ridge on Bugaboo. We stood there as it slid all the way down to the lowered glacier. Back at camp, everyone told of their day's climb and more drinking followed up.

After the Bugaboos, Billy learned that Urs had made the first ascents of the north faces of Mount Victoria, above Lake Louise, and Mount Athabasca, on the Columbia Icefield. Billy was inspired to find his own big mountain line in the Rockies.

Chapter 6

MOUNT ASSINIBOINE
AND BILLY THE EDITOR

Some rocks were covered with ice, which made climbing
very difficult, but on our descent the sun had turned the
ice to water, and we got several shower-baths. There rocks
were very rotten and interspersed with patches of snow
and ice... Having no lantern with us, we hurried on, as
we did not want to be benighted on the mountain, but the
loose stones made care necessary.
—GERTRUDE E. BENHAM, AFTER CLIMBING
MOUNT ASSINIBOINE (1907)

THE WIND RATTLED THE SCREEN DOOR OF
Archie Simpson's southeast Calgary house at 4503 First
Street. A late-summer high-pressure system was holding
over the Rockies. Billy arrived at Archie's house late in
the afternoon. It was September 1969, and they were
preparing to climb Mount Assiniboine, the tallest peak
in the southern Rockies. Commonly referred to as the
Matterhorn of the Rockies because of its resemblance
to the famous Swiss peak, Mount Assiniboine was first
climbed in 1901 by James Outram, Christian Bohren

and Christian Hasler. The name derives from an Ojibwe word for "stone boilers" and was used by Europeans to refer to the Nakoda people. It's remote and dangerous, and climbers had died trying to climb it.

Billy and Archie were motivated by Brian Greenwood and Jim Jones's new route on the north face of Mount Temple. It was a kilometre-high alpine route on decomposing stone capped with an ice sheet and double-knifed cornice. Billy had climbed Mount Temple earlier in the summer with 23-year-old Don Gardner via a snowy east ridge. Born in Calgary around the same time as Billy, Don started climbing at 13. A brave climber inspired by the solos of Walter Bonatti, he joined the CMC in the 1960s and spent most of his time in the mountains with Charlie Locke and Chic Scott.

Billy and Archie would go on to spend a week making their first ascent on Mount Assiniboine. The steep east face had one "easy"-looking passage but had never been attempted. Reaching the base takes climbers through dense forests and past scree-covered alpine meadows. Archie had visited Assiniboine in the winter of 1967. On December 20 that year, along with Brian, Chic and Eckhard Grassman, he left the Three Sisters Dam at Bryant Creek on the Spray Lakes Road on a snowmobile, towing the others on a sled as they held their climbing gear tight. They made it to the warden's cabin and continued on skis. They were hoping to find the Naiset huts, but in the -35°C weather, they decided to break into the Assiniboine Lodge for shelter. The following day, Charlie Locke and Don Gardner arrived after skiing nearly 40 kilometres during a chinook and blowing snows. They skied together to the base of the mountain across the frozen Lake Magog on the 22nd.

Charlie didn't like the weather and turned back to the cabin. The other five climbers strapped on crampons so their feet wouldn't slip off the ice-covered rock on the north ridge and continued up. Unfortunately, the competitive side of Don and Eckhard wasn't welcomed, and as they moved ahead, with Chic behind, Archie and Brian turned around. Archie and Brian weren't into racing up the mountain. Chic, Don and Eckhard reached the summit, unroped and turned around. Using the rope for the descent, they were forced to sleep in their bulky sleeping bags. With snow filling their sacs, they suffered through a miserably cold night. Everyone saw each other on Christmas Day at Brian's, where they drank and ate roast duck. There were no hard feelings.

Archie knew his way into Assiniboine, but he and Billy couldn't employ his snowmobile because of mechanical issues. The line on the mountain they were to follow had ice, snow and loose rocks on ledges. The golden-hued larches in the distance resembled a burning forest. As the sun rose, they started from their bivy at the base of the face and climbed blocky limestone. To the left and right were glaciers; the sound of the collapsing seracs echoed in the alpine amphitheatre below. Billy had never been on such a remote alpine climb, but he had no difficulty finding sound stone to place pitons. They alternated who climbed first. At half-height, they found a ledge where they slept and melted snow for water. They'd been in the shade for most of the day and were chilled to the bone. Billy awoke before sunrise in anticipation of the heat a rising sun would bring.

As they climbed higher, the rock got colder. Loose stones fell from overhead and ricocheted down to the glacier below. On the cusp of the summit of the 3618-metre peak, a snow squall came from the west. The temperature was below zero as they stood on the summit and brewed tea. It was the first time both climbers stood on the summit, from which you can see the Bugaboos, Mount Temple and the Goodsirs. Their route was the hardest climb on the mountain. They downclimbed the north ridge and camped again before making the long walk out. Billy wrote a two-page story about their adventure, but it got lost in the trove of CMC memorabilia. Archie wrote a short summary of the climb that he mailed to the *American Alpine Journal* for the 1970 volume:

> Mount Assiniboine, East Face. On August 31 and September 1, Bill Davidson and I made the first ascent of the east face of Assiniboine. The route follows a prominent rib straight up to the summit and avoids the iced walls which impressed Chris Jones. The rock is average for the Rockies, some very rotten and some reasonable. There were several good pitches of about F5. Few objective dangers threatened on the rib, apart from two precariously balanced 15-foot ice mushrooms. The glacier at the bottom of the face is the worst I have been on in Canada and so axes are recommended. The route is more enjoyable than the northeast ridge except for a couple of hours of bad brush from the Wonder Pass trail to the head of Lake Gloria.

* * *

The CMC had a regular newsletter that had been going out to members for years, summarizing club events and mountain climbs. After their Assiniboine climb, Archie suggested to the club that Billy take over as editor, and they agreed; Billy already owned a typewriter. Until Billy, a newsletter was a single page, short on actual news, and always listed club members. Billy introduced poetry, stories, rescue reports, listings of gear for sale and more. Archie became the assistant editor, and Billy moved into his spacious house. Together they created newsletters that helped bring awareness to the new generation of climbers. Billy would write creative pieces like:

> George and Bill went up the hill to do a bit of trundling. The boulders came down all around, Christ, what a Sunday. Trundling, for any of you unfamiliar with English culture, is the art of rolling big stones down hills or over cliffs, eh George.

In his December 1 newsletter, Billy included a calendar listing for a slideshow by Ron Smylie about climbing Mount Logan, and a ski movie. Two weeks later, another newsletter promoted avalanche courses, more slideshows and a party to be held December 19 at Brian Greenwood's: "Party at 616 30th Ave S.W., bring $2.00 to pay for the kegs and food."

In the four-page January newsletter, Billy included a poem and trip reports from Murray Toft and Dick Lofthouse. In the February edition, he listed the committee members, included another announcement of a party at Brian Greenwood's and provided a schedule of films playing. On the last page was a list of potential new routes on Yamnuska, which at the time had only 20 routes.

The route dream-list had been written by Billy and a few other club members at a pub that winter. Typically, rock climbs are named by the first people to climb them. The grades are attributed after the first ascent. In the 1960s, rock climbs were graded with three ratings: the commitment level, measured on a Roman numeral II-to-VI scale; the aid climbing grade, from A0 to A5; and the hands-on-rock free climbing grade, measured on the F-scale between F2 and F10. The F-scale was later abandoned for the Yosemite Decimal System. This was the list that Billy published in the newsletter:

A would-be climber's guide to the Yamnuska

Central Buttress V A4 F9

The rock between Calgary Route and Direttissima. Follow a line of corners through belts of overhangs. Extensive aid climbing to grey slab.

Suicide Wall VI A5 (sustained)

Or III A1 if a bolt ladder is used. The big face to the right of Direttissima.

Kallenwand IV F9 A4

Solo the first three pitches of Grillmair. Move left and climb the steep corner, using aid for the upper part. Move left and climb to Chockstone Corner to a final corner.

Grillmair Route III F9

For the person who hates chimney, climb the Grillmair to ledges and traverse left to steep corner.

Burp Crack V A5 F8

Start as for Outer Edge, but two rope lengths below
the pinnacle, traverse right on a large ledge for 80
feet, this ledge continues to Forbidden Corner. Climb
the wall above to a good ledge below a tenuous crack
system, the somewhat unfortunate use of bolts has
to some extent simplified the climbing problems
encountered in that crack. Above is a very prominent corner which completes the climb.

Bowl Direct V F10

Sustained free climb for a bold leader. Climb the
centre of the arch below the bowl. A small buttress
marks the start of the climb, which continues to the
top of the Bowl.

Yellow Edge V A5 F9

The prominent buttress bounding the Bowl on the
right. Start by a corner, F8, and continue by a series
of increasingly difficult corners to the right of the
main buttress.

The April 1970 edition included a poem that
maybe best conveys the spirit Billy brought to the
CMC newsletter:

Archie Simpson lying in bed
Hears a ringing in his head,
Opens an eye, picks up the phone,
Some of our boys may never come home.

Brave Howe and Woolie Lamb
Are trapped by dark upon the Yam,

Twas simple Slymon on the line,
Come quick, come quick, there may still be time.

Leaping up, he starts to dress,
On with tie, there may be press.
Up went the rockets, out went the call,
Don Bolokoff, Brian Warpwood, John Furtin and all.

On top of Yam, prepare the winch
And a volunteer who will not finish.
Bold half gallon over the edge,
Down to the victim on the ledge.

Soon the boys are safe from plight
And as the sun gets rid of night,
They gather round and as a team,
They fart in unison, "God Save the Queen."

Chapter 7

SQUAMISH

The basic difference between an ordinary man and a warrior is that a warrior takes everything as a challenge while an ordinary man takes everything as a blessing or a curse.

—CARLOS CASTANEDA

AT THE TURN OF THE DECADE, YOUNG CLIMBERS were becoming regulars at campgrounds around Canada and the US, and climbing journal articles, which had once ignored how climbers *felt* and focused only on what they *did*, became filled with expressions of emotion and ambition. The CMC had become more than a group of rookie climbers led by Brian: it was now a pack of experienced alpinists who'd frozen their toes on big mountains and forged new routes up scary walls. More climbers moved to Calgary in 1970, like Brits Gerry Rogan, Jack Firth and Bugs McKeith and Canadians Tim Auger and Pat Morrow. It was a collection of some of the best climbers in North America. One of the climbs that proved the club's standards had risen was Ray Breeze and Jeff Horne's rare ascent of the Beckey/Chouinard in the Bugaboos.

The towering granite alpine climb had only a few repeats before them.

In the spring of 1970, the CMC started weekly visits to a large boulder, a glacial erratic called Big Rock, in a flat field south of Calgary. There, climbers trained technical skills without using ropes on the short problems. They wore frayed bell-bottomed jeans, tie-dyed shirts and headbands. Billy often wore a fringed buckskin vest. They would start on the easiest route, which was called Beginner Slab, climbing up and then down the problem. Billy's favourite climbs were the Overhang Direct and Archie's Special, the most difficult and tallest rock climbs on Big Rock. After their visits to the boulder, the climbers would walk back to their cars with grass-stained pants, bloody hands and torn shoes, and drive back to Calgary for pub night.

That same spring, the CMC had started to revitalize an abandoned forestry hut on the eastern shoulder of Yamnuska. The hut would become a base camp for climbers exploring the valley behind Yamnuska, which became known as the CMC Valley. The first climber to explore the area was Fred Roth, who soloed new routes in the 1960s. After a few days of clearing deadfall from around the hut, Billy and other CMC climbers uncovered four walls and a collapsed roof. They fixed the roof and added support beams. Within two weeks, the CMC hut was finished. Urs later donated copper plates from his printing press for the roof shingles. Billy wrote the following about what would happen if non-climbers arrived:

Club Member: "Hello, are you members?"

Young man: "No."

Club Member: "Good, then we can leave it locked."

Young woman: "Do you mind if we eat our sandwiches on the porch?"

Club Member: (With a little hesitation) "I think that would be OK."

As CMC climbers were pushing limits in the Rockies, a group known as the Squamish Hardcore were doing the same on the west coast. The Hardcore subscribed to the philosophy of "hard living and hard climbing" set out by west coast climber Gordie Smaill. The club included Steve Sutton, Hugh Burton, Neil Bennett, John Burton and Greg Shannon. Their logo was an apple core, and they spent as much time in the Chieftain Hotel pub as on the rock.

By the time the Hardcore arrived, climbing in Squamish was well established. The main focus of attention was the Chief, a hulking mass of rock that towers over the town. It started to draw attention in the late 1950s, and in the summer of 1961, Jim Baldwin from Prince Rupert and Ed Cooper from Seattle became the first climbers to scale the biggest section of the face. Their ascent was covered by national newspapers. The first few pitches were tucked behind the tall trees and no one took notice. That changed as soon as one of them could be seen above the treeline with a rope dragging behind. At one point, 12,000 people gathered to watch them. Newspaper headlines read, "Two Climb, Thousands Watch." The men admit that, with so many people watching, they felt obligated to reach the summit. This was no easy feat, as the rock face had many surprises in store. Halfway up the wall is a pillar of rock detached from the most solid face, which became known as the Split Pillar. The pillar vibrated and expanded when Jim and Ed hammered pitons behind it. They then encountered an exfoliating flake, the size of a small building, which rattled when struck with a hammer. The flake became known as the Sword of Damocles and almost caused them to stop the climb. After 40 days of effort, they finished and named it the Grand Wall.

The Grand Wall was climbed again by Vancouver-based Tim Auger and Dan Tate, who were both teenagers. In 1964, they spent two days on the Grand Wall before escaping on the Dance Platform, a treed ledge near the top. At the same time, Americans, including the famous Fred Beckey, were travelling to Squamish to climb untrodden stone. The next serious route up the Chief, University Wall, was climbed by Tim Auger, Dan Tate, Hamish Mutch and Glenn Woodsworth. They followed a steep corner that often seeped, far left of the Grand Wall.

In 1963, Jim Baldwin wrote the first rock climbing guide to the area, *A Climber's Guide to the Squamish Chief Area*. It was handwritten and later typed for publication, but Jim died in Yosemite the following year, and the guidebook was never released. Jim had rappelled off the end of his ropes under a dark sky after climbing Washington Column. His death was considered one of the biggest losses to Canadian climbing. It wasn't until 1967 that fellow Squamish climber Glenn Woodsworth produced the area's first published guidebook.

An overhead view of the Chief reveals not a solid bulk of granite but rather three summits with ridges, ribs and faces that hide deep gullies. The Apron is a slab of cracked rock that protrudes from north of the Grand Wall. In the summer of 1970, Steve Sutton and Hugh Burton climbed a new route on the Apron which they called the Grim Reaper. The angle demanded them to fully trust the rubber on their feet as small crystals dug into their fingertips. The protection was far apart, and a fall would result in some serious road rash. It wasn't climbed for another ten years. Between spouts of hallucinatory drugs, the pair climbed three routes on the Chief that summer. The first was called Uncle Ben's, a new route next to the Grand Wall. They used bat-hooks to aid on small edges and brought enough beer for the ascent. The next route was their new Zodiac Wall, found in the north walls and climbed over two and a half days. Their third was a would-be third ascent of the Black Dyke that was thwarted by injury.

As they made their way up the Black Dyke, Billy was high on the Grand Wall, making an early repeat attempt. He had acquired a copy of Woodsworth's guidebook from someone at the CMC and decided to make his first trip to the west coast. Billy, Brian Greenwood, Stu Stymon and Archie Simpson squeezed into Archie's Bronco for the overnight drive. Once they arrived in Squamish, as Billy later wrote,

> we went straight to Tim Auger's house to get his iron from the Chief. After coffee at Tim's somewhat elegant mansion, we headed for the Chief. A traffic jam, due to a line up for the ferry, caused us to arrive somewhat late in the afternoon. We rounded a corner and there was the Chief. It looked rather frightening, towering above us.

On the road into the camping spot, we found John Moss hibernating in his sleeping bag. He had driven from Edmonton with a friend. After getting established at camp, we made a recky of our individual routes. Brian, John and Archie were planning to climb Tim Auger's University Wall, while Stu and I had a look at the Grand Wall. Both are somewhat over 1,600 feet and mostly aid climbing. After a short scramble, we stood heads bent back, staring in awe at what was before us. We quickly headed back to camp. I was captivated by the ocean.

Next morning saw a frenzy of activity. Can you believe that? Piles of gear were being sorted. Stu and I had some 40 carabiners and 50 pitons to carry up. After reaching the base, Stu and I scrambled to the top of a large pinnacle. I dropped down some forty feet and started up a bolt ladder. Three leads on bolts and we found ourselves below a huge right-facing corner or pillar. The bolts were fun, some 320 in all. About here we heard a crash. Later we found that some people on the Dyke Route (next to ours) had dislodged a large block onto one of their member's hands. He was taken to the hospital and they continued with such phrases as "What? Yea, real neat." The route is graded A4.

The next lead went up into the corner, til I ran out of bongs. I belayed Stu up on a bolt, so he could take out all the gear I had placed. Above the bolt the crack widened out to about 2.5 inches. We had nothing of this size and had to retreat. We were up some four pitches. Down below we ran into Brian and company. They also ran into difficulty about two leads up and had to retreat. There was nothing left to do but go back to camp and have supper, then go to the bar in Squamish.

The next day was spent on small climbs which were neat, yeah real neat. Things were a little under-graded, what we called 5.7, they called 5.3. On a small route called Tourist Delight, we had all reached the first belay, but no one could get any higher. Then a group of local climbers arrived. They seemed to have been following us around all weekend and stood in the parking lot watching us. Brian seeing this made a desperate effort to get up and he did! I followed, barely, and John came up and took the biners off the running belays. One more route was done that day, Slab Alley. A local had offered to guide us up it. He ended up not leading one pitch and when he did climb, he used the leader's rope continually.

The next morning, Monday, we headed home. Nothing of any great importance happened, except one thing which sticks in my mind. Brian was driving at his usual rate of speed, somewhat over the limit. We had just managed to pass an eight-car line when we came to a hill. Sure enough, we slowed down and were passed by all the same cars. Down the other side we passed them all over again. This went on for some time, until we were at the front again and one of the cars came beside us and they held out a piece of paper with "Stupid" written on it. "One of these days, I'm going to get a car that will go from 0 to 100 in 10 seconds," Brian said.

*   *   *

Back in Calgary, Billy and Brian went straight to the Empress. They pushed the battered steel door open into the smoke-infused bar that always reeked of spilled beer, damp terry cloth and greasy food. They sat at a table with Urs, who had recently hiked to the base of Yamnuska and spotted a new climb. Urs and Brian made a plan to try the route in the morning, and Billy told everyone about his inaugural trip to the Chief.

The following day, Urs and Brian climbed a new 100-metre route on the east end of the mountain. The route wasn't big in Yamnuska terms, but it was looser than most routes and finished through a roof that drew the climber out over hundreds of feet of air. They called it Smeagol. It was Brian's last new route on Yamnuska and was the final route logged into their new guidebook: *A Climber's Guide to Yamnuska*. The small book had just over 20 pages; half of the routes were Brian's. It capped off his successful career of new-routing on Yamnuska. Years later, Urs printed a second edition, which had 34 routes. Urs wasn't finished on Yamnuska that summer and soon made the second ascent of Balrog with George Homer. Then Jack Firth and Jeff Horne made the third ascent, Billy and Ian Heys made the fourth ascent the following year. Urs and Billy then teamed up to become the third party up Corkscrew.

Urs encouraged Billy to go back to the Squamish for the Grand Wall. He said that he'd lend Billy any pitons that he needed. As Billy and Jeff Horne prepared to return to the west coast, they made the third ascent of the Bowl, a scooped wall on Yamnuska's east end. The next day, Billy teamed up with George Homer for a climb up Pangolin, a series of hard-to-read cracks near Smeagol.

*   *   *

Having climbed more than anyone else on Yamnuska that year, Billy left for Squamish again in late June. He later recounted the trip — and accompanying drunken shenanigans — in rhyme:

Return to the Chief

1. June 20th to 28th was the time, Squamish was the place, Stew, Jim, Jeff and myself, were out to gain the face.

2. The Mach 1 roared, while someone in the back snored, finally Vancouver in sight, should be on the cliff by night.

3. The Mach got gas, and we some Uncle Ben's, then off to buy pegs, just down from land's end.

4. Finally to the Chief, where big walls call, I was too pissed to hear them at all.

5. The sun rose slowly, so did I, Jim and Stew had their plans — the Grand Wall or die.

6. Jeff and local with rope in hand, walked up Slab Alley, Jeff thought it was grand.

7. Stew and Jim returned that night, for big wall climbing, Stew didn't feel right.

8. The next few days, free climbing prevailed. First Unfinished Symphony, then lots of ale.

9. The Dyke Route was fun, my camera took a fall, it decided it was done, made it for last call.

10. Try as we may, we could not find, I was afraid, would have to leave behind.

11. Stew had his troubles, later that night, the Mach 1's right window, scattered itself over the campsite.

12. The next morning, Jim and I were on the Grand Wall. The Split Pillar was reached, in no time at all.

13. I nailed the pillar, everything was going fine, Jim jumared up my fixed line.

14. Jim took the next pitch, while I hauled the sack, I heard his voice above, this is no damn A1 crack.

15. Below like ants, people stopped to stare, the view out to sea was beyond compare.

16. And so the day went, the sun began to die, upon a small ledge we were forced to lie.

17. From Black depths, a light signal cried, my one-eyed headlamp, sent back a reply.

18. Morning found us on Dance Platform's left side, above the Roman Chimneys soared to the sky.

19. Climbing was moderate till high in the chimney, an A3 crack, the pegs were flimsy.

20. Tied off blades, sweating hands, woops, there goes a peg, Jim — watch where it lands.

21. Finally a belay cave, I light a fag, sixty feet to go, we've got it in the bag.

22. Jim nails the last crack, soon we're on the top, smoking a cigarette, we admire the drop.

23. Up reaching the camp, we heard a cheer, now something to eat, and lots of beer.

Chapter 8

EL CAPITAN

Real adventure is defined best as a journey from which
you may not come back alive, and certainly not as the
same person.
—YVON CHOUINARD

RETURNING FROM SQUAMISH, BILLY PROVED
that he could go from granite big wall aid routes to
leading thin ice under snow thousands of metres above
calving glaciers. He joined Ian Heys, John Moss and
Oliver Woodcock for the third ascent of the 1961 route
up the north face of Mount Edith Cavell near Jasper. The
big icy wall was first climbed by Yvon Chouinard, Fred
Beckey and Joe Faint; in 1967, Royal Robbins had soloed
it without ropes in the only other ascent to that point.

John Moss, who would go on to climb many big routes
in the Rockies, including the first ascent of the wildly
overhanging east face of Mount Babel above the pristine Moraine Lake with Brian Greenwood, wrote the
following in the *Canadian Alpine Journal*:

> After a late start, a bivouac was taken at about 500
> feet below the top — the summit being reached the

next morning. The lower part of the face is not sustained, with only one pitch of F8 standard. The angle of the face then eases, giving some scrambling and finally very enjoyable climbing on good rock. If the prominent rib is kept to in the upper part of the face then the climb is virtually all on rock with only a few snow and ice pitches. Objective hazard was low apart from the central part of the face. The climb is extremely enjoyable, and with an early start could be completed in one day.

To follow that up, Billy set out, only two years after his first technical climb, to solo-aid one of the biggest walls in the Rockies. It had never been attempted. With some friends, he made the long hike to the north face of Gibraltar Mountain in Sheep River Valley, southwest of Calgary. He brought 100 bolts, 60 pitons, 50 carabiners and a 15-pound homemade hammock, along with four gallons of water and clothing. It took three people to carry Billy's gear to the base. Billy belayed himself with a dead-man, a self-belay system, and managed to get two rope lengths up. As he later told Urs:

> On some wet rock, I slipped and fell 100 feet. I was bruised and bleeding and alone. I could not afford to go on. I roped down and hitched a ride home. You should have seen the look on the people's face who picked me up. Seven stitches later, we returned to get my gear.

Later that week at the Empress, Ann Woolcock and Diane Homer removed Billy's stitches.

Urs, meanwhile, was in the US. He was climbing with Royal Robbins at the famed climbing destination that would offer Billy a whole new venue to expand his skills: Yosemite.

*   *   *

The sport of big wall climbing using aid techniques had started in Europe at the turn of the century. A big wall is any mountain face that requires special skills and equipment to climb and can take a number of days. In North America, big wall climbing started in Yosemite in the 1950s, led by a climber named John Salathé. John realized the big walls in Yosemite could be climbed using direct aid and then-new rope-climbing techniques. He was the first ever to craft pitons using high-strength carbon steel, which he got from a discarded Ford Model A rear axle. He used the pitons on new rock climbs like Lost Arrow Spire in 1946. John arrived in Yosemite at the dawn of a new era of postwar outdoor recreation in North America, in large part driven by people going to the mountains.

A few years later, a young Californian named Yvon Chouinard was taught by the Southern California Falconry Club how to rappel from cliff tops. Yvon enjoyed it so much, he and his friends hopped freight trains to climb at an area called Stoney Point. He also joined the Sierra Club. Yvon soon moved to Yosemite to learn about big wall climbing. He needed new climbing gear, as there wasn't enough to go around, so at 18 he walked into a junkyard and bought a used coal-fired forge, a 138-pound anvil, tongs and hammers, and taught himself how to blacksmith. He made his first pitons from an old harvester blade and, with T.M. Herbert, tried them on Lost Arrow Chimney and the north face of Sentinel Rock. Once word spread that Yvon was making chrome-molybdenum steel pitons, he was in business. He could forge two pitons an hour and sold them for $1.50 each.

He forged pitons through winter and climbed in Yosemite in the spring. When it was too hot, he travelled to the high mountains of Wyoming, western Canada or the Alps. In the fall, he would return to Yosemite until it snowed. In 1965, he went into partnership with fellow climber Tom Frost, an aeronautical engineer. For nine years, they would return from the mountains to redesign and improve their climbing tools, to make them stronger, lighter, simpler and more functional. By the time Billy started climbing, Yvon's company, Chouinard Equipment, was the largest supplier of climbing hardware in America.

It was rock climber Warren Harding, however, who Billy most idolized out of the Yosemite climbers of the 1950s and 1960s. Warren had been dubbed "Batso" for his ability to spend so much time on a big wall, and for his radical character. He developed specialized equipment for climbing, such as the bat-tent for sleeping and bat-hooks for hooking precariously small cut-out bits of granite. They were part of his Basically Absurd Technology (BAT) product line. He began climbing in the Sierra Nevada in the late 1940s. After he started technical climbing in 1953, he quickly proved himself to valley locals. He was shorter than most other climbers, drank a lot of wine and liked fast cars. In the 1950s, Harding pioneered nearly 20 Yosemite big walls. The most impressive and famous of his ascents was that of the Nose in 1958. The route was Warren's answer to Royal Robbins's big new route on Half Dome.

In July 1957, Warren started up the Nose, a huge buttress feature on El Capitan's central line, with Mark Powell and Bill "Dolt" Feuerer. El Capitan rises from the valley in such an awe-inspiring way that it's maintained the title of the most sought-after big wall in the world since it was first climbed. They fixed ropes that they could later climb to easily reach their high point. Low down on the route, they were thwarted by wide cracks. To protect the cracks, they used wooden legs from a stove that Frank Tarver had given to Warren. They also hammered prototype bong pitons into the rock. The cracks became known as the Stove Legs Cracks. In 1958, Warren, Wayne Merry and George Whitmore finished the climb, hammering their way up the final pitches. Warren struggled for 15 hours on lead and placed 28 expansion bolts by hand. It was a painstaking feat to hand-drill holes in El Capitan rock. It took 45 days to climb the Nose over two years. Throughout the 1960s, Warren continued climbing new routes.

The first Canadians to leave their mark on the valley walls visited in the early 1960s. Jim Baldwin made the first ascent of the nearly kilometre-high Dihedral Wall in 1962 with Ed Cooper and Glen Denny. It was wildly steep and ahead of its time. In 1969, Gordie Smaill and Neil Bennett climbed the south face of Washington Column, the west face of Leaning Tower and the Kor/Fredericks on Sentinel Rock, and made the first Canadian ascent of the Nose. Smaill and Seattle climber Al Givler spent four days climbing Salathé Wall, a route that would later share pitches with Freerider, which Alex Honnold free-soloed decades later. Tim Auger, who'd just moved to Calgary from Squamish and was at the beginning of an impressive career, climbed Washington Column with Mike Wisnicki and then broke his ankle in a freak fall while attempting the Rostrum. He recalled hearing the bones break.

The 1970 season started when Smaill and Ron Burger climbed the Steck/Salathé on Sentinel, followed by the west face of El Capitan. Then Smaill and Neil made the fifth ascent of the North America Wall. Then Hugh Burton and Steve Sutton, both 17, arrived from Squamish and teamed up with Dan Reid for a Canadian ascent of the Nose over three and a half days. That summer, Brian and Tim teamed up for an ascent of the west face of El Capitan over three days.

It was July 1970 when Urs left with his baby, Nadine, and wife, Gerda, in their Volkswagen van for the valley. The drive took them a few days, but they'd packed plenty of cheese and wine. Once there, Urs and George Homer climbed the Direct Route on Washington Column. Urs then teamed up with Royal and climbed Chingando, a 50-metre crack. Urs tore some skin from the top of his left hand and bled into the crack, but Royal urged him to continue. Then George and Tom Evans climbed the aesthetic northwest face of Half Dome over two weeks.

Urs and his family lived in their van at Camp 7. Every night, he and the other Canadian climbers would gather around the picnic tables, sort their gear and share dinner. The usual climber's camp was Camp 4, but it had been closed as part of a park rangers' crackdown. The park had become a well-established gathering place for young people in the late 1960s, and the wardens had grown tired of their antics. Problems between Yosemite rangers and the growing crowds in Stoneman Meadow began over Memorial Day weekend 1970, when rangers fielded numerous complaints regarding loud music, drug use, fights, profanity, nudity and public sex in both Camp 14 and Stoneman Meadow. The climbers did their best to stay away from the disputes; they were focused on challenges higher up.

That fall, Billy made his first trip to Yosemite. Together with Brian Greenwood, John and Janet Moss and "some girl from Montreal," he went first to visit a friend in Seattle, where they climbed Outer Space on Snow Creek Wall, which he described as "graded 5.9, but I led it so it must be easier." When they arrived in Yosemite, Billy, Brian and John climbed Braille Book on Higher Cathedral Rock, which "had blood all over it because the day before, there was a big fall. A guy had to be rescued and his ropes were still hanging there." He and Brian roped up for an attempt at the Nose, but weather forced them down from a ledge known as Dolt Tower (so named because Bill "Dolt" Feuerer had once been prusiking downward from it to reroute some fixed ropes when he got his beard stuck in a prusik knot). Billy impressed Brian with his aid climbing skills, and Brian later said that Billy's repertoire of tricks had surpassed that of anyone else in the CMC. The pair also spent three days climbing the south face of Washington Column; as Billy would later write in a letter to Urs, "It was unusually hot then and we ran out of water for the last day. It was pretty rough! I got a little pissed-off after that and didn't do anything for a while but get drunk! (ha! ha!)."

Meanwhile, Dan Reid was looking for a partner willing to join him on another significant climb. As Billy put it in his journal,

Dan Reid had been searching all over camp for someone to do the N.A. [North America Wall] with him. Tim Auger had asked how long he was going to stay. "Oh, I'll just try once more today, then go home if I can't find anyone," he replied as he turned away. In my half-conscious state something clicked in my mind. N.A. Maybe I could — no, I'm not good enough, look Bill, they're just human like you, but Robbins, Frost, Chouinard, Pratt and the rest; they're — oh hell, I'll give it a try. "Hey Tim, could you introduce me to Dan," I asked as I crawled out of my pit.

The North America Wall was already one of the most sought-after big wall routes in the world. First climbed in 1964, it was only the third route up El Capitan, after the Nose and Salathé. It followed a swerving line of cracks and roofs up the southeast face. Some of the best of the golden age of Yosemite climbing — Yvon Chouinard, Tom Frost, Chuck Pratt and Royal Robbins — were among the first to climb the route, which represented a big leap forward in style and ethics. As Billy would later confess to Urs, the sight of this monumental wall left him "scared shitless."

It's funny how news travels in camp 4. By noon Dan and I had a large crowd around us as we sorted out vast amounts of gear. Our friends helped us carry the gear up to the base of the wall. We needed help!

Eighty pounds of water, food for eight days, three ropes, and more iron than I had ever seen before. MMmm — the hauling was going to be a real gas. On the way up, we came across Warren Harding, below the Wall of Early Morning Light. After an exchange of good-lucks, we continued up to our line.

Warren Harding and Dean Caldwell's ascent of the Wall of Early Morning Light would go on to become the most difficult rock climb yet accomplished. It followed cracks between the Nose and the North America Wall and took 27 days to complete. They had set off with 300 pounds of food, water and gear, enough for 20 days. They placed hundreds of bolts to overcome blank sections, along with bat-hooks and rivets. They got trapped in their bat-tents in a four-day storm. On November 11, the National Park Service had to rescue some climbers on El Capitan and hinted that they wanted to rescue Warren and Dean. Warren dropped a tin can with a note that read, "A rescue is unwarranted, unwanted and will not be accepted." They reached the top on November 18, sparking a media storm.

That ascent is one of the most famous Yosemite stories ever. Little does anyone know that Billy and Dan were on the North America Wall at the same time and weathered the same storm as Warren and Dean. They also called off a helicopter rescue.

These troubles were still remote, however, when they reached the Gulf of California ceiling and Mazatlan ledge, where they spent their first night on the wall.

As I munched on some tuna, I heard Dan on the two-way radio, calling his friends below. "Base to portable N.A. Wall, read you loud and clear Dan," crackled back the reply. These radio calls were something I really began to look forward to. We received nightly weather reports and one night the air was warmed by music from a tape-recorder.

The next day included a 5.8 squeeze chimney and a difficult pendulum to Easy Street ledge, and they spent their third day on the wall getting to Big Sur ledge.

There was a big flake, 5.7 climbing, which posed some problems for the hauling. We got to Big Sur early, so we decided to fix the first pendulum. This pendulum and the following nailing are as well-known as the third pitch — in being horrible.

I had visions of swinging clear of the wall, as Dan pulled me in on the hauling line. I had a fag to calm my nerves, then started up. From some bolts, Dan lowered me till I was about thirty feet to his left. He locked the climbing line with a jumar clamp, and began to haul me in on the hauling line. He then let me go, and I swung far left, trying to grab a flake. However, my feet, which were supposed to be clear of the wall, got in the way, and I swung short of the flake. One more try and I managed to grab the flake. I heard a distant cheer and, looking below, I saw a huge traffic jam and crowds of people.

The flake curved upwards to my left and petered out into a hair-line crack. Above the crack there was a three-bolt ladder. Moving up on sky hooks and tie-offs looped over chipped parts on the flake, I got up to the crack. "Wooee — what a mind blower," I yelled.

If I came off here, I would really swing. I placed a
rurp and climbed up to my second steps. Still being
short, I placed knife-blade and tied it off. It started
to shift under my weight, so I drove in another blade
behind it. Slowly I stepped up till I reached my
second steps. Still too low! "Watch it Dan!" Top steps
— still too low — Christ, how did Frost put that bolt in
— MMmm place a tie-off over the stack — put my toe
in the tie-off — inching up — watch it Dan-ya man,
I've got you sweating crab off — damn hanger — click
— "Whoo-Weee, that was hairy Dan, I'll belay here."

That evening, on their weekly radio call with friends,
Dan and Billy learned the storm was on its way.

They said it would probably arrive sometime tomorrow night. Well, we should be in the Black Cave by
then and could wait it out there. The next morning, I
jumared back to the station pulling the hauling line
with me. Dan then let the bag out with the third rope
and I hauled it up. Dan tied onto the climbing line,
fixed his jumars to the line, rigged a rappel with the
third rope and rappelled off of Big Sur ledge. When
he was below me, he pulled the rappel line down. WE
WERE NOW COMMITTED!

But the sanctuary of the Black Cave was farther
away than it looked. The final push to get there brought
another heart-stopping event:

The third pitch was awkward, over-hanging and
leaning right. It was one of those greasy-type cracks

with a lot of gardening to do. About 30 feet up a pin pulled out and I found myself across from Dan and about 15 feet out. He pulled me to the high-point. When I saw what held me, I nearly had a heart seizure! It was a leeper, good old leeper, in about a half an inch and tied-off. I placed a pin and climbed up to my second steps. No sooner had I got the next pin in when the same pin pulled.

This time Dan was ready and stopped me ten feet down. I could just barely get back in to climb up. I finally reached two bolts and belayed. It was getting late — one pitch to go — Dan got to me as it was turning dark. By headlamp he started off — getting cold — down jacket time — curses from above — head-lamp not working right — cigarette glowing.

"I'm up! Hey man, is this cave weird, no floor in it." As I cleaned, I could hear Dan calling to his friends with the radio. "Portable Black Cave to base — over — crackle crackle — hey Bill, they want to know how you're doing," Dan shouted down. "Just fine," I yelled. Was it ever weird to be cleaning in the dark! My headlamp revealed two-inch-long centipedes running in and out of the crack I was working on.

I finally got to the cave and found water bottles and gear hanging all over the place. After getting into my hammock we had something to eat. The rest of the time we spent listening to the bats flying around in the cave. In the morning I woke to a terrific view; 2,000 feet of air below my hammock. I noticed the clouds hanging low in the valley. Once in a while a spire would poke its way into visibility through them.

But they did not resume climbing that morning, as heavy rain forced them back into the cave.

All that day and the following night. I was getting hammock sores, and worst of all, I was out of fags. Dan found a broken part of a fag in the day pack. "Oh man — that's good!"

The morning found me leading left on shaky pins. It was our fifth day on the wall. After about fifteen feet I started up and slightly right. It went faster due to a lot of free climbing. Dan led to the Cyclops Eye, our next bivy. We had time however, to fix the next two pitches: the first an A4 traverse right for forty feet to a corner. The next went up the corner for a rope length to some rooves. As Dan finished the corner, the weather started to deteriorate.

Back down on the Cyclops Eye we rigged a plastic sheet. It really rained that night but we kept dry. We heard over the radio that a party on the West Buttress had to be rescued and that they were thinking of coming for us as well. "The hell they will!" Dan called back. They also clued us in on Harding's progress. He was moving very slowly.

The next morning saw us at our high point. A sky-hook move got me over the first roof to a bolt. Here we heard a shout from below and turned on our radio. "Really looks good Bill," came the distant voice. I looked down and perceived a group of ants by the road. "The rangers are here again and they want to know if you're all right?" "Ya, We're all right. We don't want to be rescued!!! We'll be up tomorrow. Are you coming to meet us? OVER." "Ya

Dan, see you tomorrow. Way to go guys. This is base, over and out."

The summit was almost within reach, and Billy was optimistic that they could get there the same day. But tricky stretches slowed them down and kept them on the wall another night.

> Two pitches to the top. So close I could smell it. But darkness was closing in. One can of fruit left.

> The next morning, our seventh on the wall, saw Dan across the second to last pitch. I quickly began to nail up the last pitch. Too quickly. A3 in an expanding crack caused a short fall. Then free climbing. Hard, steep, and lots of rope drag. Short of the TOP. Dan flies up to me and leads on. He's there. Now I'm moving; faster than Dan can pull in the rope. Better be careful.

> The top, hand shaking, congratulations, fags, oh beautiful fags, champagne, food, tears of joy, picture taking, snow starting to fall, 5 mile walk off the back, but it didn't matter, we made it.

Writing to Urs a year later, Billy described his return to camp: "Everyone was saying, 'Who is that guy?', 'What has he done before?', 'I have never heard of him, have you?'"

It was a truly remarkable achievement and helped cement Billy's legend. As Royal Robbins had said of his first ascent of the North America Wall, it was "the climb of our lives. More difficult and more serious than anything we knew."

Or, as Billy summarized it in his letter to Urs, "It was a real mind blower."

Chapter 9

NINE NIGHTMARISH NIGHTS ON NOTHING

*Difficult experiences are the way we learn, and they also
are the way we can appreciate ease. We understand bright-
ness by its contrast to dimness, happiness by its relationship
to sadness. By embracing this duality of experience, we
allow ourselves to find peace within our difficulties rather
than wasting our power on trying to escape them.*
—ARNO ILGNER, THE ROCK WARRIOR'S WAY

It doesn't have to be fun, to be fun.
—BARRY BLANCHARD

IN JANUARY 1971, BILLY WAS BACK IN CALGARY,
saving money for a new camera and preparing his
slideshow on the North America Wall for the CMC. He
kept busy writing letters to friends. Near the end of
the month, he wrote a letter to Urs, who was visiting
Switzerland. After recapping his Yosemite feats, he
brought his friend up to speed on local developments:

> I don't know if you know or not but we have a real
> nice hut now behind Yam. There have been a lot

of new routes done now. I am working on a super route, on the most overhanging wall behind Yam. It is about six hundred feet high. So far, I have used 21 bolts (that must be a record). George [Homer] and I went into the Bugaboos to do Snowpatch East Face, but as usual, bad weather screwed us up.

At Okotoks Rock, there are lots of new routes up. Remember the real overhanging wall at the back by the fire (the one you and Brian were chipping away a hold?). That's been done now lots of times. I have even done it!! There is another route just to the left of that and many other elsewhere. Well, that's enough about climbing (not bad for one summer, hey! Ha! ha!).

I have just been lazing around since Yosemite. I have not been working on anything (what a bum!). I have decided to stay in 16mm filming. I have ordered another Bolex, $2,000 worth. It is a reflex with variable shutter, 400-foot magazine, a motorized zoom lens, electric motor, batteries and everything. What do you think of that? I hear you got a new projector. Great! What kind is it? How's my old camera doing?

We still enjoy our Wednesday night outings to the Empress bar. Hey, guess what? We have up to now had three free rounds from the Empress (they must be really hard up!). Brian has been fired from Premier Sport. Too much pool and not enough work, I guess. I have applied there for the job but do not know yet if I have it. Just think, me as the climbing salesman (and after all I have swiped there! Ha! ha! ha!). In one week, I am showing my slides on the N.A. Wall at the club. Should be a packed house! I have about 100 slides on the N.A. They are really good. The place hasn't been the same around here without you, Urs.

*   *   *

In the spring of 1971, Billy hitched a ride to the Yamnuska parking lot. From there, he hiked to its base and then continued west. After a few hours, he reached the bottom of a rising buttress on Goat Mountain. He slept in a forest of lodgepole pine trees below the rocky prow. In the morning, he started climbing, solo, with 600 metres of rock above. Nearly 100 metres off the ground, a simple rope error led to his dropping his hammock and haul bag. After a hasty retreat back to the ground, he packed up for the day and returned to the city.

In Calgary, he recruited George Homer and Jeff Horne for another climbing mission. They made their way to the Archie Simpson hut a few days later. Billy wanted to complete a steep buttress in the CMC Valley known as Wakonda Buttress. The name came from George seeing Billy on the wall alone on a previous trip and saying, "There's my *wak on the* wall" (in British climbing circles, "wak" meant "buddy"). Having tried the route alone, Billy invited George to attempt the first ascent of the exposed aid climb with him.

Billy and George completed the route and named it Iron Suspender. The 240-metre climb started with two hard aid climbing pitches that led to easier free climbing. Billy wrote about their ascent in the Archie Simpson hut logbook:

We got to the hut late Friday night. Our spirits soared high that night as the weather showed signs of promise. What's that saying? Red sky in the morning, red sky at night, it doesn't matter, we'll still get pissed tonight. The next morning, we got by with a little help from our friends. Jon Jones and Jeff Horne helped carry the huge pile of gear up to the wall. Picture taking, sorting, smoking, posing — all part of the overhanging wall.

Jon and Jeff soon leave and we are left with our thoughts. That fixed rope had been there since Christmas. Sure George, you can jumar first. Up go the bags — very slowly. My turn. Wild — the wall is about 15 feet way; life is that red tattered line slashing the incline. Finally, we both sit on the first ledge. Well, what are we here for anyway? Get the rag out. I start up. I climb to our high point. Blank. Out comes the drill. George is below getting a sun tan — tap tap tap tap — in goes a small aluminum stud. A stainless steel wire hanger. That won't hold. It does. A knifeblade. Two sky hook moves. Rope drag. Finally, a good crack and the end of the second pitch.

George lets the haul bags out and as it soars out some 30 feet, he shuts his eyes. Man — that's overhanging. George leads the next pitch. It is very short, but makes up for it by being very hard. When I get to him, it is hammock time. The lug frowns upon us as we munch on some tuna. The night passes reasonably well — my foot keeps getting into George's mouth.

The second day on the wall sees George climbing free up to the lug (ear). I wonder if it can hear us.

"The left side won't go man — I'll try the right. Hey! I need some bongs." (B.O.N.G.= Bang On Nothing George.) George finally gets to the top of the lug and up goes me and the bags. I gear up, look up, light up and finally start up. The first move is a sky hook which tries to be an eye-hook. "Place a bolt Bill." I get onto a ramp which leads left freely and then the ordeal. Bolts, bolts, bolts, somewhat short of a rope length, I come down for our second night on the wall. Astride old lug, shouts from below, good God, there's an army down there. Fraser, Noodle (the valley is still echoing), Jon, Jeff and I can't make out the rest. Soon they leave, we try some reading. No good. Into our hammocks. I see a bat. Sleep.

As the sun slowly rises, so does George on our high point. Little shiny specs mark his passage. After sky-hook, free and bolting, he makes a seat belay. The little pitter-patter the lug hears slowly fades away. I start the second last pitch. Hot, this is no fun in the sun climb — I feel faint. Haul up some water. On I go, finally free climbing. We are going to make it. Belay. The last pitch looks a piece of piss. As George comes up, I hear a shout from above. They've come up to meet us. Damn. The haul bags stuck. George jumars down. Up come the bags. The last pitch wasn't done in great style, we wanted off... I pull over the top to come eye to eye with a 50 mm lens. George follows. Hand shaking. Jeff Horne goes down and climbs back up with the haul bag on his back — thanks man. On the way down, we had a good trundle, but I won't speak of that now — this is neither the time nor the place.

This has been a Billy Davidson Epic Production. Starring CMC and featuring Wakonda Buttress and filmed on location at the hut.

On April 7, Billy teamed up with Jeff Horne. They hiked through a forest of poplar and aspen trees to the trail below Yamnuska and walked west looking for a weakness to climb. They found a depression up a steep, loose section of gently overhanging rock. It rose above the trees towards the east end of Yamnuska. It looked to be about 200 metres, not blank and possibly climbable, but too loose to aid climb. Jeff and Billy would have to rely on their free climbing skills. As Jeff applied pressure to the rat-piss-covered rock walls in the lower chimney, big blocks of sharp limestone broke away. The depression they were climbing was a band of weak, rotten rock, which had been eroding away for thousands of years. At the top of the first pitch chimney, Jeff belayed Billy up while sitting on a sloping ledge. Billy then climbed left onto a steep wall, where a row of perfect handholds revealed itself. He barely made it to a small ledge before he ran out of rope.

The next pitch was easier, but the rock was stacked like cards, so Jeff climbed quickly. Billy then took an hour to dig a tunnel-like groove up the next pitch. He eventually found rock good enough to take a piton. They had trundled thousands of pounds of rock by that point, "enough to fill a Volkswagen Beetle," Billy later said. The fifth pitch was an awkward traverse; Jeff nearly fell off the mountain when his ledge broke. With the cloud of dust from the broken ledge came the smell of sulphur. Billy took the final pitch. The 50-metre rope-length was like a stack of China plates. There was no protection, and when one of Billy's handholds broke; he swung away from the wall like an opening door. His other hand stayed firmly attached, but he told Jeff that he was properly "freaked out." He wanted to go down, but they couldn't, it was too dangerous. Billy reached the top and sighed with relief. Brian Greenwood described the route in the *Canadian Alpine Journal* as "a nasty line between Corkscrew and Pangolin." Billy and Jeff named it Freak Out.

The following week, Billy teamed up with Jim White for another attempt on Mount Gibraltar. Jim didn't know what he was in for. No one had attempted the wall since Billy tried the previous year; which left him bashed and bloody. With a friend identified in Billy's account only as "Sharon," the two set off for Mount Gibraltar, which proved to be the challenge that Billy was looking for. Afterwards, safely back in Calgary, he wrote the following account, which he called "Nine Nightmarish Nights on Nothing":

> I felt my foot slipping—damn rain! Rock and sky became one big vertical blur—the next thing that registered was a tightening around my chest. There was blood all over the rock and on everything else. The belay plate had worked or I would have sailed 150' instead of just 120. I managed to get back to a ledge upon which to reflect on my misfortunes. DOWN BABY, SOLOING'S TOO DANGEROUS!
>
> That was 1970. A few stitches and the North America Wall later found Jim White and myself back for more. More of what, I don't know. Perhaps if I knew, I wouldn't have to do stupid things like climbing.

Gibraltar had not changed. Still smiling down upon us minute mites, its upper lip formed one of the biggest overhangs I have ever seen.

"Ah—we'll piss up it," I said as we searched for reassuring gestures from each other.

We didn't have a good start. Car trouble, bad weather, bloody heavy loads to carry up to the base. We fixed the first pitch, which I couldn't remember from last year, and returned to see Sharon off. Then back up to see the sun hightailing it westward. You know, the usual garbage. Oh, how beautiful it is—peace of mind—wish I had a joint.

The morning dawned fine or did it? I don't remember. Should have made notes. The next few days mainly involved hauling our two bloody big bags up the slabs. I suppose we did some climbing as well, but the hauling weighed heavily on our minds. For the most part, the whole climb is vague in my mind. I think I could give you a menu for our suppers though. No? Well, let's see now. We made very slow progress. Would you believe two pitches a day. I remember Jim doing a lead in 20 minutes. Two hours later we got the bags up. Fun this climbing. Maybe the English have something when they revolt against this sort of game. The bivys were great. On the second day my hammock opened its mouth and nearly swallowed me up. I retaliated by shoving it into the cavernous pit of the hauling bag. Belay seats from then on. Higher up the technical difficulties increased, A4 to open a tin of tuna, but the hauling got easier.

The weather was always bad. Snow, storms, lightning, rain, cold winds, belay from pits and jackets, and all this on a north face which got the sun only a couple of hours a day. Below us the route stood out in bold relief. Piles of—well piles and pink paper, all the way up to us. What's all that stuff about dropping something from the top and that's the line to take. Forget that—just follow the droppings, that's the line we took. I won't bother with the usual trivia about how we nailed this, freed that, jammed this, squeezed that, and bolted here, bolted there, and generally screwed around everywhere.

If you want to know what it's like, do the damn thing. Every night we would have visitors on the wall and down below. It would come from the east, a sort of—well it sounded like a tractor in need of a tune-up—Sharon's car. She screamed; we screamed; not the generation gap, just the distance.

Our wall visitor was in the form of a little furry ball of hair. What it saw was two funny animals in need of a wash. Piles of coloured things all over the place, and look at that. A long blue worm coming up the rock. I'll just take a bite; they won't miss one little bit out of 165'. The next morning Jim cried.

On the second last day, I was doing a Warren Harding on a smooth bit of rock when a shout caused me to look down. Jim pointed towards the top. Sure enough, a hairy head was peering at us over the edge. "Hello—who are you?" we said to John Martin. He said "How are you guys doing?" Ug—moan—gasp—ugg—gronk. "Will you get to the top tomorrow?"

The next morning—bolts, bolts and more bolts. "How are you doing Bill?" Ug—gasp—bang—bang—gasp. Upside down bolting, dust in the eyes, clear air below, wanting just to get off and finally doing so.

John and Sharon have come up to meet us. That was really nice of them. It's some slog. It begins to snow. Bang, bang, bang — a quick bolt and Jim came up. Sigh of relief from below. Jim had belayed me for five hours. John and I haul the bag hand over hand—no use bothering with proper style. Jim gets up. We shake hands, say smagma, click and down we go.

Driving out we looked up at our battleground. Still aloft and more mysterious than ever. It had not been changed by the mere presence of man, but we had. We were pissed off with climbing.

The route was never repeated — no one was interested. Billy had brought big wall aid climbing to the Rockies, but this wasn't Yosemite, where the granite was more conducive to that style of climbing. Aid climbing on the limestone walls in Alberta was dangerous, and the rock was unpredictable.

A week after the historic first ascent on Gibraltar, Tim Auger, who was soon to be the backbone of Banff National Park, teamed up with Don Vockeroth for a new route on Yamnuska. Billy was in the hut when he heard about Tim and Don heading up and hiked over to the forest below to watch. Don had attempted the route before; it was the one that Billy called "Burp Crack" in his list of unclimbed routes in the CMC newsletter. Don and Tim spent the day climbing to the top and named it Kahl Wall. "It was breathtakingly exposed, more than the Chief," Tim said. "From the high-point I stepped out onto the blank wall and find small edges the skin on my fingers gripped. I slotted a hex into a water runnel and moved upwards. We only aided a small bit." The route became one of the most classic 5.10 rock climbs in Canada.

Shortly after Kahl Wall, Billy returned to Yamnuska to attempt to solo the Super Direct, a route that Brian had named for its positioning directly below the summit, where the wall was highest and steepest. Billy had already made several attempts with others, but never alone. He climbed to a new high point after finding a thin crack, where he hammered in narrow pitons. He turned around in a rainstorm and rappelled down fixed ropes that were soaked through. The next morning, Brian and Don hiked to the hut, where Billy was drying his gear. They brought him food and wine. Billy continued climbing for the rest of that summer. In the fall, he was appointed vice president of the CMC, George Homer the president and Jeff Horne the treasurer. He never did complete his Super Direct solo.

Chapter 10

CMC WALL

We came again and again, and each time this mountain
became dearer to us and each time our ties grew more
intense... We could appreciate the friendly sunlight, we
could appreciate a little ledge to sit on, we could appreci-
ate the encouraging handshake of a friend and we were
ready to trust each other, help each other and give to each
other our everything... This mountain teaches us that we
should endure hardships and that we should encounter the
difficulties and not drift along the easy way, which always
leads down.

—HANS GMOSER, ON YAMNUSKA

IT WAS A COLD JANUARY DAY WHEN BILLY
heard that Archie Simpson had died in a climbing
accident. After arriving in New Zealand the previous
year, Archie had teamed up with a local climber named
Austin Brooks. They made the first ascent of Mount
Dixon's west face up what they called the Left Buttress.
A few days later, Archie achieved his goal of climbing
Mount Cook, the highest mountain in New Zealand.
While descending from the summit, he fell to his death
between the Haast Ridge and Tasman Glacier. Archie

was the CMC president for 1969 and 1970, so in his honour, the CMC renamed the Yamnuska hut the Archie Simpson hut.

That same month, Billy visited the Empress with Brian a number of times. One night, two young men walked in and sat two tables away from Billy. They looked like climbers. Billy shuffled his chair over to say hello. One of the young men was John Lauchlan. He'd just moved from Winnipeg and had started going to high school with CMC climber Gary Jennings. The other was Jim Elzinga, a tall, rigid-jawed Calgary-born climber who was wearing Wrangler jeans and a denim jacket. Gary, Jim and John were members of what would become the Junior Boys' Choir club, the next generation of Canadian climbers. They went on to make many first ascents in the Rockies and focused mostly on cold, icy mountains. Other climbers in the club included Rob Amman, Mike Sawyer, Bruce Keller and Darrell Jones.

By April, Billy was working part time at Premier Sports in Calgary, selling camping and climbing gear. Rumblings of a climber named Charlie Porter were making their way around the climbing circle. He was said to be the next big wall climbing superstar after Warren Harding. Another young CMC climber at the time was Ken Wiens, who would one day go on to be the club's president. His introduction to climbing came one fateful day at the climbing shop where Billy worked. Decades later, he wrote a letter to Rob Wood about his first introduction to climbing through Billy:

> As a 16-year-old fresh back from my first Columbia Icefield ski trip, I wandered into Premier Sports one afternoon to pick up a replacement burner

plate for the one lost from my Svea stove. I walked to the counter and met Billy. He told me about hard rock climbing, the CMC and falling. He pointed out pictures on the walls of routes he had done (and some he had fallen down). I listened for two hours mesmerized about the thrills climbing could provide.

As Billy talked, he brought more and more gear off the shelves and placed it on the counter. Finally, he attempted to close the sale of over $1000 of gear (remember this was over 30 years ago) only to discover I only had $5.00 in my pocket. He decided that was close enough, packaged the gear up and out I walked adorned in a multitude of pitons, carabiners, slings and a hammer. I forgot the burner plate.

Billy had instilled such a longing for adventure that climbing became my life for the next 25 years. I never saw Billy again after that first day (although I dropped into Premier several times looking for him), but as I met more and more members of the climbing community (aka CMCers) I soon discovered that he was a technical and "spiritual" leader in the colourful collage of people that lived to climb.

That spring, Urs returned after two years in Switzerland climbing classic routes in the Alps, such as Pfaffenhut on the Wendenstöcke. He and Gerda had married there, where a wedding was cheaper than it would have been in Calgary.

Billy wasted no time in connecting with him. It was a rainy afternoon in April when Billy visited Urs, bringing him a used television. Calgary was expensive for newlyweds; with two young daughters, Urs was tight for cash.

He would go on to use that TV for 20 years. While Gerda stayed home with the kids, Urs got a job at a graphics company; there was money to be made in print media, and he wanted to learn the trade. Billy and Urs made a plan to head back to Yamnuska once the weather improved and attempt a first ascent of the Super Direct.

They had to wait until June for good conditions. A few days before their departure, Billy called Brian to ask him along. After all, this route was Brian's idea, and he had made the first attempt on it, with Urs in May 1968, only to be rebuffed by a snowstorm. Brian was eager to come and asked to bring Tim Auger too. Billy obliged, but with misgivings he would later describe in his journal:

> Deep down inside I wasn't at all happy about that — nor was Urs. The three of us had spent many days fighting our way up to where we felt confident on a push. Was this Tim Auger going to get the tender meat without first tasting the gristle? I could just be feeling jealous; Tim is a hell of a good climber. Anyway, as in most things, I found it hard to say no.

The morning arrived. Billy and Urs grabbed coffees before leaving Calgary and headed for the mountains; Brian and Tim would meet them there. The sky was dark blue, the mountains snow-free and the fields green from weeks of rain. Everything Billy had practised, all of his knowledge, was about to be put to the test. He and Urs hadn't climbed together since their last time on Yamnuska, two years prior. Billy had new pitons forged by Yvon Chouinard and a daisy chain of carabiners. Urs had a selection of new European hardware, including a light hammer. They would never be more ready.

While Billy waited at the first ledge for Brian and Tim to show up, Urs went to work above him. He was starting on their second fixed rope when:

> Far off, I perceived two tiny figures making their way along the faded path. I waited at the first ledge till they came within shouting range.
>
> "Hey Brian, are you guys still coming up?" Silence. They appear to be discussing the situation; finally — "No — all that jumaring looks like too much work."
>
> "Well," I replied, "could you untie the bottom line so that I can pull it up?" As I watched one of the little figures move cautiously up to the base I felt suddenly relieved. That cleared the air, so to speak. I think Brian knew how we felt. I still feel bad about that. I wish Brian could have come along.

After a day of intermittently challenging climbing — "I can never get used to this damn stuff," Billy wrote, recounting an incident that saw him swing out suddenly — Urs and Billy bivied in their hammocks. Day two presented formidable obstacles:

> I light a fag. Above and to the right the next set of roofs looms above us. They don't look very inviting. First of all, a delicate traverse is required to get into them. Oh well, I start across. Turns out to be pretty thin nailing. I don't envy Urs having to clean. Arriving back in the middle of the corner I decide to tension down and right outside the corner. I get to a small ledge and can see it looks a lot better than all those roofs above the corner. I belay.

Instead of jumaring across, Urs climbs it as I belay. He's pretty psyched out. I don't blame him. It was a bloody good cleaning job. Urs asks me to lead the next bit, so I start up. It's now steep face climbing and quite enjoyable. After a short run-out I decide to place a belay bolt. The drill (used on the Iron Suspender and Gibraltar) finally decides to break.

I screw around awhile and get something to work with Urs' kit. We take a long time. Urs is getting fed up and so am I. The constant pressure of a new route and the scorching Albertan sun is taking its toll. We hear some noises below and yell down to some guys returning from a climb. "Hey you guys — our bolt kit broke. Tell Brian to come up with a rope," Urs yells. The little figures run off along the path to the parking lot.

Above me an ugly crack arches left. Well, may as well keep going — it will make for less of a distance to lower the rope. About halfway up the crack I begin to feel a little better. We can't use the self-drill anymore, but Urs has these Leeper bolts and a drill. They will do for belays, we hope. Limestone is a lot different from granite. Those bolts don't work as well as self-drills. My thoughts are interrupted by a shout from below. It's Brian, our out-of-breath guardian angel, with nothing we can use.

"Are you guys alright?"

"Yes, I guess so — but you better come out in the morning to make sure."

I reach the end of the crack and put two Leeper bolts in for a belay. It's getting dark and cold as Urs starts to clean. That night we munch on some tuna and peas.

The morning of our third day finds Urs placing rivets up a bulge and diagonally right. Sometime later he comes back down. "Hey man, how about you finishing off the ladder, I'm just dead." I'm tired of sitting in one spot and grab the lead eagerly. Too eagerly — in my haste I drop my bat-tent; the one I spent months making. Never did I find it.

The pitch ends on a fairly good ledge with a good crack above. We're getting close. I can't get very good bolt, but manage to smash in some reluctant pins. It's funny how you trust belays more while standing on a ledge than in a hanging position. One gets funny ideas about holding the second and hauling the bag even if everything spills.

After Urs reaches me I start up the last bit — really nice nailing, then a rotten section. Traverse left to another groove, then free up over some loose stuff to a long roof and left to a belay.

Urs reaches me and I am ready to go again. It's getting late. A couple of rivets get me to some free climbing. Up a chimney, its huge mouth full of loose teeth ready to spill out, and suddenly — the top!

Can't find anywhere in the scree to put a pin. A loose knife blade is used to tie the hauling line off. I grab the climbing line and belay Urs who climbs instead of jumars. We both pull the bag up hand over hand.

The first ascent of the Super Direct was complete. It had required every skill Billy and Urs had learned over the years, and they were both exhausted. They rechristened the route with its new, official name: the CMC Wall.

They carried their gear off the mountain, down a slope and through the forest. The gear was heavy, a hundred pounds of iron and rope. They left their climbing gear in the woods, next to a spring, and walked to the highway. They slept under a piece of cardboard until they got too cold and hitchhiked home. Back in Calgary, Billy convinced his girlfriend, Sherilyn, to drive him back to the spring below Yamnuska. He wanted to retrieve their climbing gear. After loading it into the car, he went straight to visit Urs and return his gear. They shared a bottle of wine and reflected on their achievement.

Billy would later write about the moment they achieved the summit:

> A very cold wind springs up. The top of Yamnuska is turning orange in the setting sun and a deep purple haze fills the valley behind. God, this is beautiful — should have a camera. No! This wouldn't look any different from any other sunset on film. Even the memory will fade in time.

*   *   *

In August, Billy and Dick Howe found themselves part of a rescue team on the East End of Rundle above Canmore. A climber fell when he got lost hundreds of feet off the ground on a rock climb known as Guide's Route. There were no topos or guidebooks at the time, so climbers went by word-of-mouth descriptions. On any big climb in the Rockies, getting lost is as easily done as said. A photo of the rescue appeared on the front page of the *Calgary Herald* on August 11.

The image was taken by Pat Morrow, who told me:

A climber took a whipper and nearly ripped his kneecaps off. There were several of us who got the call and responded, but just Billy and Dick are in the pic. Fellow climber Steve Jennings drove his busted up old car up the dirt road at 100 miles an hour to get us there. We were part of the volunteer association, the Calgary Mountain Rescue Group. I was 17 when I first met Billy, in the bar at the Empress hotel where the Calgary Mountaineering Club hung out. I never did get to climb with him, but enjoyed his stories in the pub and admired his fearless approach to what amounted to the hardest test-pieces of the day, done in an understated manner befitting a member of the CMC.

Chapter 11

HALF DOME

Hour after hour feeling with fingers in the darkness, bad
cracks, shifting pins, pins coming out, too steep to go
down, bashed fingers. I didn't care. I was as far along the
thin edge as I wanted to go, digging it and hating it, and
finally finishing it, but not enjoying it... But certainly, if I
had it to do over again, I would.
—*ROYAL ROBBINS, ON TIS-SA-ACK*

HALF DOME IS A GRANITE MONOLITH THAT
rises above the eastern edge of Yosemite Valley. Three of
its sides are rounded and one is a flat face that makes
it appear like the dome was cut in half. Historian and
naturalist John Muir wrote about Half Dome in his
1912 book *The Yosemite*, in a chapter called "The South
Dome." He talked about how a trail-builder named John
Conway attempted to climb Half Dome in his bare feet
in the early 1880s. Conway occasionally drilled eye bolts,
which he would fasten a rope to for protection. The
upper part of the smooth dome required many more eye
bolts than he was willing to place.

The iconic peak was first climbed in 1875 by George
Anderson, who drilled eye bolts into the rock every few

feet. He would then pull himself up and stand the highest one. Muir wrote, "Occasionally some irregularity in the curve, or slight foothold, would enable him to climb a few feet without a rope, which he would pass and begin drilling again, and thus the whole work was accomplished in a few days. From this slender beginning he proposed to construct a substantial stairway which he hoped to complete in time for the next year's travel, but while busy getting out timber for his stairway and dreaming of the wealth he hoped to gain from tolls, he was taken sick and died all alone in his little cabin." When roped climbing in Yosemite was started in 1931 by Bestor Robinson and Richard Leonard, it was declared that Half Dome's big wall was "so awful it might as well be forgotten."

The first ascent up the steep northwest face of Half Dome was in 1957 by Royal Robbins, Jerry Gallwas and Michael Sherrick. It took Royal and his team five days to climb the 650-metre wall on gently overhanging rock. Jerry hand-forged much of the hardware they used for the climb. In 1958, Michael wrote about their ascent for the *Sierra Club Bulletin*:

> Some have said that we did the "impossible," and it is unfortunate that for decades the world impossible has been such a common term in the mountaineers' vocabulary, being applied to that part of the mountain which presents an extreme in difficulty too demanding for the equipment and technique of the day. Big improvements in technique and equipment just keep on happening.

In 1969, Royal was back on Half Dome. With Don Peterson, he spent nearly a week climbing a new

650-metre-tall route, which Royal called Tis-sa-ack. Royal tried it the year before, but retreated from just below halfway up the face at a platform known as Twilight ledge. The route was one of the hardest big wall climbs in the world and one of Royal's proudest efforts.

In September 1972, Billy took a bus to Yosemite. He would later write:

> The bus trip was desperate. All the way down I was continually psyching myself up. The climb? To solo the second ascent of Tis-sa-ack. It had been tried by many a good hand, but they all came off with horror stories about loose flakes and desperate pitches. Why then was I trying it solo? I could give the usual answer, but mainly I knew what it would mean if I succeeded — FAME! It is hard to admit this, but I think that reason moves many onto desperate routes.
>
> It rained the first couple of days but finally I started taking gear up to the Dome. It took three days to carry all my gear up there. That, I think, was something in itself. Forty-eight bloody miles. A hard way to get fit. I also carried up 50 pounds of water only to find the spring below the face still running.
>
> The first pitch ended on a good ledge, but I had a hell of a time trying to find where the damn thing started. Robbins' description said "wander up several moderate pitches to the Zebra." I know there's a lot of controversy about having too lengthy a topo, but Robbins went to the opposite extreme. I mean, six sentences for a route of that size! He

probably did it with good purpose in mind — he would have been happy to see his route unrepeated ten years from now.

Anyway, I got all fouled up in this A4 stuff. After placing a poor angle, I tied off a small bush and clipped into it. No sooner had I done this than the angle pulled. The higher I climbed the worse things got. Five feet below the ledge everything went blank. The ledge was round and sloping so hooking was out of the question. I screwed around a while then finally placed a rivet and did a desperate mantle to gain the ledge. Christ — some moderate pitch! I left the pitch fixed and went down to the valley to recharge my keenness batteries.

Back at camp, Billy learned that he was too late for the second ascent: Charlie Porter and Jack Roberts had done it weeks earlier.

Oh well, a third ascent solo is better than nothing. A day's rest and I was back on the first ledge. The hauling was terrible. The next pitch was alright, save near its end where I tried a fairly hard free move and ran out of slack. When you get near the end of a long pitch the weight of the rope pulls back any slack you make to do a certain move. So, I had to back down and take in all the remaining rope and tie it off. Then with twenty feet of slack, I reclimbed the free part. It was late in the day by the time I got everything onto the Dormitory, a huge ledge below the Zebra. I fixed part of the first lead into the Zebra and came down for the night.

As the sun sank below the bald head of El Cap, I reflected upon the events of the day. Looking up I tried over and over again to follow the line of the route. My body was tired but my mind wouldn't stop working. During the day's activities one has no time to ponder nor worry about things ahead. Only the placement just above. But at night all one's fears and speculations come boiling to the surface. Sleep was a long time in coming.

He set out again the next day, with help from an innovation of his own:

The third day saw me at the first station in the Zebra. The hauling was now a lot easier, due to the increased angle of the wall. With all three lines hanging properly I started up.

Three lines — yes three — climbing line, hauling line and IRON LINE; a new invention of mine! This allows me to carry only a small portion of the iron needed. The rest hangs at the station on a fifi hook attached to the rope. When one needs some iron one has only to haul it up, take what one needs then leave it hanging on the peg below. It worked quite well. (Patent pending!) Saves sore shoulders from the weight of 84 pins.

There was an awkward spot in that lead, but finally I got to a small ledge formed by a large flake just below the loose section. From that ledge a huge ear-like flake stood up away from the wall, twelve feet high. Above it there seemed more of the same. When I placed a four-incher behind it the ledge I was on vibrated. I decided to give the bong one more bash for good times sake. That was a bad mistake. The blow must have loosened a flake higher up. It hit me in the back of the head. IN SOLID YOSEMITE ONE NEED NOT WEAR A HELMET! There was blood all over the place, and my courage was flowing out with it. Down man, before you kill yourself.

That was easier said than done. It was some six hundred feet up. The Zebra slanted right. It would be hard getting to the Dormitory.

He rappelled, a bloody mess, from old slings left from a 1971 attempt by Peter Haan.

On the rappel to the Dormitory I ended up 20 feet above it. There was nothing else to do — hanging onto the pull line, I just let the rope run through the brake bar. Sudden rush; hard landing; grabbing for anything so as not to bounce off the ledge.

So ended the solo attempt.

After stewing awhile at camp and contemplating going back home, Billy found a partner willing to make another bid for the third ascent: Mike Breidenbach, nicknamed "Figgy," who had just climbed the Salathé Wall.

We reached my previous high point on the second day and I tried that loose bit again. Chouinard Hexentrics and hooks got me over it, but God was it freaky. Fig led to the top of the Zebra and I started the next bit. I got across the five-inch crack without incident. The A5 flake was next. A knife blade stack and No. 1 stopper got me to its top. I was shaking like a leaf in a storm. Where's that damn bolt? — Oh yeah — I remember someone telling me that the second ascent party took the hanger off. I finally spotted the stud sticking out and got a tie-off over it. Then there was a short bolt ladder and I belayed at its top.

The rest of the route is just one big horrible blurred image in my mind. I do remember that it was continuously hard. Figgy tried to free the first five-inch crack. Near its top he came off and nearly ended in my lap. Then on a reverse under an upside-down expanding flake, I took two bombers. On the second five-inch crack, also expanding, Figgy made the mistake and tried to place a pin. The result, a thirty-footer. There was a guy soloing on the Normal route, and later he told me how he would hear a scream and see one of us plummeting through the air.

Late on the fifth day we got up to the last pitch. I decided to fix as much as I could before dark and then we could get off early the next day. It was bloody awkward, and being without food and water for two days didn't help things much. Luckily it was cold or we would have had another epic like the one on Washington Column.

That night we had a smoke to ease the pain. It began to rain a little later and we prayed that the weather would hold. It did, and we finally got off that dangerous mother. We didn't expect anyone up to meet us, but my good friend Tim [Auger] arrived with water, food and all the necessities. I had more than dirt in my eyes as we shook hands and embraced each other.

When word of Billy's ascent of Half Dome reached Calgary, Urs wrote in his own journal, "Billy is a big wall man, none of us dared dream he'd ever go this far."

*　　*　　*

After Tis-sa-ack, Charlie Porter and Gary Bocarde climbed a new A5, the most serious of all aid grades, which they called the Shield. They used 35 RURPs, the smallest pitons on the 40-metre-thin Triple Cracks. A few weeks later, Charlie completed the first ascent of Zodiac Wall, solo. It would become one of the most classic big walls in Yosemite. He named the route after the Bay Area's Zodiac Killer, who claimed victims during each of Porter's attempts. Charlie's impressive ascents were casting a shadow over any other climbs done at the time, including Billy's.

In Urs's view, however, Billy's achievements were not overshadowed. "Billy Davidson," he later wrote, would "become the Charlie Porter of the north. They both were loners and both pushed aid climbing to new standards. They were in a league different than the rest of us."

Back in Calgary, Billy moved in with his dad and looked for a job. The next CMC night at the Empress, he ran into a friend from Wood's Christian Home, fellow climber Perry Davis. The two got jobs at Crane Supply. For the next year, Billy stayed busy working as a construction labourer. He bought a red Honda motorbike

FROM TOP   Ron Nesbit and Ken Davidson at Camp Chief Hector in 1960. *Photo by Billy Davidson*; Hiking up Three Sisters from Spray Lakes in 1965. *Photo by Bruce Millis*

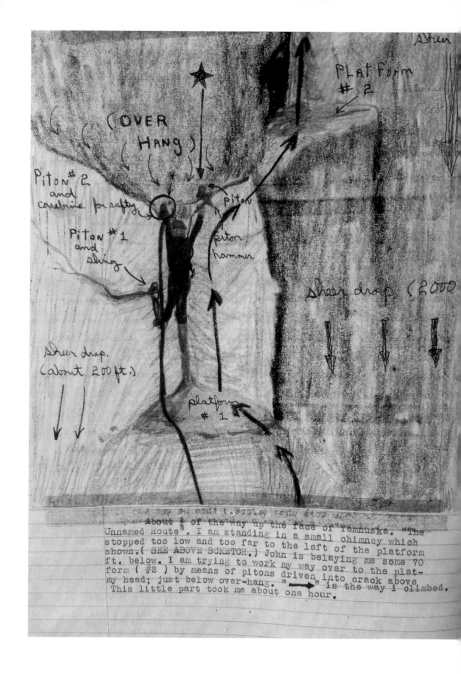

Aid climbing demonstration for crux of Unnamed Route
on Yamnuska in 1967

FROM TOP   Billy on the first ascent of CMC Wall. *Photo by Urs Kallen*; Billy and Gary Jennings on top of El Capitan. *Photo courtesy of Gary Jennings*

Billy high on Yamnuska. *Photo by Urs Kallen*

Billy before the climb, wearing his piton hammer. *Photo by Urs Kallen*

Billy and Rob Wood on *Shadowfax* during their
maiden voyage.

FROM TOP   Billy paddling through a storm. Painting by
Billy on Stewart Marshall's art studio wall; Kayak Bill in
1988. *Photo by Jim O'Donnell*

FROM TOP   An early painting where tape was used to
create the lines; Zig Zag man in an eye

FROM TOP   Raven on a log; Ravens similar to ones Billy
would include in his climbing journals

FROM TOP Moody weather at an unknown location;
Bird's eye view of a point that Billy had never seen
from above

FROM TOP   Granite and ocean at an unknown location;
Magical west coast scene at an unknown, possibly
fictional, location

A warm sky with weathered trees

FROM TOP   One of Billy's camps years after his last
visit. *Photo by Jon Dawkins*; Another of Billy's camps.
Photo by Jon Dawkins

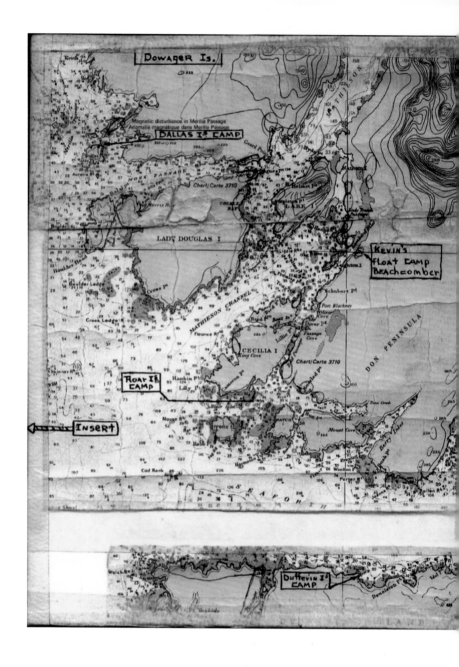

Camps on Dallas Island, Roar Island and Dufferin Island,
and Kevin's float camp where Colin Lake met Billy

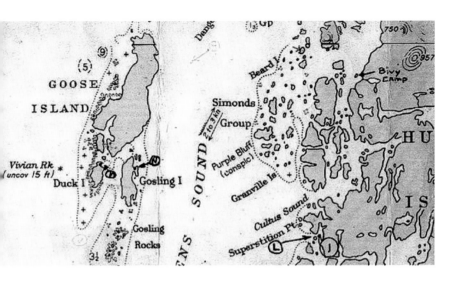

SUNDAY	MONDAY	TUESDAY	WEDNESDAY	THURSDAY	FRIDAY	SATURDAY
	1 PD#8 — 4 scatt. thin Cld.w/L.E→SE — HIKED to Is. off SE Pt. (stashed FW). — M.OC. by even w/M→Str.SE. *WORLD AIDS DAY — Bruce Peninsula and Fathom Five National Parks established in Ontario 1987*	**2** —OC w/ E→LE SE & Sprk. —LSE w/M→HR by late AM. —Lots FW work —SCATT. TH Clds (→SW) by EVEN (Str. dur Sqalls)	**3** —M clr.w/ LE→NE. HUNTED +5. Pt. (deer seen) —M OC by EVEN w/M→Str.E →SE.	**4** —OC w/M →Str.E→ NE & Sprk. —Spells of day w/ NORM L→MR thru SE (Str→E) by EVEN. PD#7 (EVEN) *Biodiversity Convention 1992*	**5** —A little clr. w/M Ly & Mixed R+ HAIL shrs. —Long hike to W. side of Is. —OC w/ M.E →SE & LR by EVEN.	**6** —O.C. w/M →Str.E→ SE & Sprk. —LR shrs. thru. day. —Lots FW work plus sweet Rice dish. —Lower back & Stomach PAINS.
7 PD#6 E6 OC w/ L. R shrs & VLVW (O.S.?) Fog/Drizzle w/LN→NW by NOON.	**8** Full Moon	**9**	**10** *HUMAN RIGHTS DAY Saguenay-St. Lawrence Marine Park established in Quebec 1997 Georgian Bay Islands National Park established in Nova Scotia 1929*	**11**	**12**	**13**

FROM TOP   Billy's chart showing Gosling Island, where he died; Billy's final journal entry

FROM TOP   Coastal weather and an unknown residence;
The location of *Ayak* after Billy's death

to ride to the mountains. In April 1973, he heard that Charlie Porter and Jean-Paul de St. Croix had completed a Royal Robbins project on El Cap that they named Tangerine Trip. Snow fell over them for a week, but the wall was so steep that they stayed dry.

Billy wasn't much interested in Yosemite anymore because he wanted to save money and move into his own place with his girlfriend, Sherilyn. He would drive to Okotoks to climb on Big Rock with the CMC and visit the Archie Simpson hut on weekends.

That October, rumours of Yosemite big wall climbs made their way north of the border. Steve Sutton and Hugh Burton, who earlier that summer had climbed a big new route up the biggest wall in the Bugaboos that they named Warrior, joined forces with Chris Nelson and Charlie Porter for the first ascent of an El Capitan big wall aid route up a blank piece of rock to the right of the Nose; they called it Mescalito.

Brian Greenwood's last serious new climb came in 1973 with Bob Beall, Rob Wood and George Homer: a direct route up the north face of Mount Kitchener. There were 30 pitches of scary alpine climbing above the 200 metres of unroped climbing up the Grand Central Couloir to gain their line; the roped pitches included six of ice that ranged from WI3 to WI5. Three pitches were on verglas-covered rock and the rest was on rotten stone. The rock was so bad that they called the climb Kelloggs, as in the cornflakes. They were hit numerous times with falling rock and ice; Beall suffered a broken finger. The route has never been repeated.

On the last day of fall 1973, Billy quit his job at Crane Supply and got a part-time job at Calgary Photo, a camera store near his house. He walked to work every day, as did Urs, through snow and sun. They said it was training for the following spring's Yamnuska objectives.

On a cold winter day, Billy broke trail through knee-deep snow to the Archie Simpson hut. The door swung open under the weight of the snow. *Thump, thump* — Billy kicked the snow off of his boots. He lit two candles and the wood stove, and then unpacked a sweater, cheese and rolling papers. He sat at the table, which he and Archie had built, and rolled Drum into brittle papers. *Thwack* — tree branches banged against the hut when snow piled on them blew off. A draft between the logs nearly blew the candles out. Billy opened the logbook and flipped through, reading stories from climbers who had visited over the previous year, including the pair of John Lauchlan and Jim Elzinga, who made the second ascent of the CMC Wall and nearly made the first free ascent.

Jan 26, 1973:

Woke up to a fantastic morning, but clouded over. Walked around the base — colder than a witch's tit. Froze my rozetas off. Star cluster was good.

—Infinitely Distant

*   *   *

June 19, 1973:

John Lauchlan and Jim Elzinga did Snakecharmer again and more or less Chingle. Hopefully back in a few days.

*   *   *

June 25, 1973:

Arrived yesterday as others were leaving. Kept awake most of the night by assorted midnight skulkers and scurryers. When I finally got to sleep, I was rudely awakened by what appeared to be a large dog sticking its head through the hole in the window and surveying the selection of eats on the counter. As I hastily arose to protect food stuffs, I became aware that my intruder was not, in fact, canine. It was comrade Blinov. He explained that he had just escaped from the Moscow circus (where he was kept in silence by a large muzzle and forced to perform unnatural acts in front of audiences) and was seeking political asylum in the cabin.

* * *

June 26, 1973:

Took a try at Iron Suspender but gave up after the third bolt. "Who climbs mountains!?" Eventually climbed Snakecharmer.

—Billy

* * *

June 27, 1973:

Decided to leave but will be back on Friday. John sprained his ankle while running down the rock scree completely out of control. Everyone will be pleased to know he gave birth to a gold ball on his ankle.

—Jim Elzinga, Darrell Jones, John Lauchlan

*   *   *

June 31, 1973:

Copped a Dirty Dago while the weather permitted.
Jim and I make the bid for CMC Wall. It's going to
be wild.

—John Lauchlan

Billy closed the logbook, shuffled to the door and
stepped out for some fresh air. He smoked a joint and
went back into the hut. A cold wind blew his candles out
before he shut the door, so Billy went to sleep.

Chapter 12

YELLOW EDGE

I still look forward to all those great new lines that I see.
And I wonder who is going to do them.
—*URS KALLEN, ON YAMNUSKA*

IN JANUARY 1974, BILLY WAS LIVING WITH HIS DAD and spent most of his time at a place called T-Square, so named because a T-square hung from a beam on the front porch. It was a two-storey house near downtown Calgary where the Junior Boys' Choir lived. The walls were painted in earth tones, and the campy furniture doubled as beds after late-night parties. Billy had exchanged his bell-bottoms for tight brown corduroy pants and grown his hair to his shoulders, and he had a scruffy moustache. He'd sit on the beige sofa, smoke joints and strum an electric guitar. One afternoon, he put down the guitar to write a poem about his climb on Half Dome, interspersing the narrative with introspective lines:

> Upon my first look
> at a face so sheer
> what was I trying to learn –
> how to control my fear?

Or was I there for
the glory I would gain?
From soloing Tis-sa-ack
Just imagine the fame

To be honest
I think a little of both
I am human
I have needs like most

The poem ended with a vow to continue with solo efforts:

It was scary and dangerous
A hell of a climb
Could I have soloed
I'll only know in time

For I have not given up
on the solo game
sometime in the future
I will try again.

One cold night, Rob Wood stopped by T-Square. Billy opened a case of beer and passed a few around. Rob sketched Billy playing guitar and told John Lauchlan a few ice climbing stories. John wanted to be an alpinist, and Rob had a lot of experience.

Billy didn't care for winter climbing but shared a love of big walls with Rob. In 1971, Rob had travelled to Baffin Island and made the first ascent of the south summit of Mount Asgard. In the Rockies, he had teamed up with climbers like Bugs McKeith, Jack Firth and Tim Auger for first ascents of dozens of now-classic winter ice climbs. The gear was rudimentary, the clothing heavy, the boots made of durable but easily frozen materials. Ice climbers in the 1970s were pioneering a sport that put them face to face with frozen waterfalls in avalanche-prone gullies on isolated mountains. For protection, they brought construction-grade rebar and metal studs.

Rob went on to write many books and journals about his exploits. "That first year I'd say we modestly seduced some of the more obvious waterfalls," he wrote in his book *Towards the Unknown Mountains.*

> We found the hard way, we had much to learn about surviving Canada in winter with its immense scale, its thirty-below temperatures, its deep, dry powder snow and, of course, the dreaded avalanche. It was common for us to take time off in the summer for our new-found sport, but Bugs and I took some time off in the winter. We lived in a plywood "bivouac box" on the back of Bug's Toyota pickup and would park it as close to ice climbs as we could. It didn't matter where we slept, it was bloody cold. As our confidence grew, we climbed bigger and steeper and more remote ice.

Just two weeks prior, George Homer, Tim Auger and Rob had climbed a huge continuous flow of ice that they named Bourgeau Left. It was an obvious objective above the Sunshine ski area parking lot, west of Banff. Rob finished telling the story about their first ascent and invited John to go for a climb. Rob was going to try to climb Takakkaw Falls, a cascading 300-metre-high waterfall in Yoho National Park. John said yes.

Brian Greenwood stopped by and hinted that once he turned 40 later that year, he was going to quit climbing. No one thought much of it. Climbers were always quitting, usually because of a near-death experience.

A few weeks later, Rob and John made the historic first ascent of Takakkaw Falls, along with Tim Auger, Jack Firth and Bugs McKeith. It was the climax of Rob's ice climbing career, but it was just the start of John's.

*   *   *

Later that winter, Billy borrowed money from a bank, sold his red Honda and bought a Harley. He couldn't afford insurance for his new motorbike, so he simply didn't get any. He spent the early March days touring the city roads between T-Square and Brian's house. One Friday after work, Billy rode to the parking lot of Yamnuska. His curly hair was pressed under his bandana as he squinted into the setting sun. He rolled a smoke and used binoculars to look for new routes in the fading light. He stayed until dusk and then rode home. He had to work the following morning at the camera store.

The following night, Rob told his friends that he was going be leaving Alberta for the west coast. A few weeks earlier, he'd met with the Canmore town council and outlined his plan to turn the small coal mining town into the future of Canadian outdoor recreation. Jack Firth dropped him off at the meeting and advised him to wear a tie, but Rob refused. The town rejected Rob's plan, prompting him to leave Alberta in search of more like-minded people. That was the last night Rob spent at the Empress with the CMC.

In the morning, Billy walked home from T-Square and thought about Rob's decision. Rob had no money and only a few belongings. Billy, now in his mid-20s, wished he could leave, but he had climbing plans. He quit his job and sold what few belongings he could to buy a bow and a quiver of arrows. He packed a small bag with pencils, paper, food and psychedelic drugs and started to walk towards the mountains. After thumbing a ride, he started up the familiar trail through the steep woods that led to the east shoulder of Yamnuska and eventually to the Archie Simpson hut. He wrote in the logbook:

Mar. 22, 1974:

Arrived with a sensation of already being here.
Crystals in the trees and silk curtains in the sky
cotton on the cliffs, smoke in my eyes.

Lumps of snow begin to grow and into mushrooms,
row on row.

I'm as light as a feather, I tell the trees so.

They ask for a dance, green hands.

EXTENDED.

I'm awfully clumsy, hope you won't be offended.

The sun is looking just over the ridge. Long sliver
threads tied to my hair or is it moss — I don't care.

—William (Acid) Davidson

In the morning, he packed his solo aid climbing equipment and made the two-hour hike to Goat

Buttress. For five hours, in the hot March sun, he climbed up the rocky prow by resting metal aid hooks into small dimples of stone. The eroded rock features made aid-hooking easy. When he came to a crack in the rock, he drove a piton as deep as he could. *Bang, bang, bang, ping, ping, ping* — the sound of the hammer hitting the metal told Billy it was safe to put his weight on. The sudden shift of any piton under his weight made his heart skip a beat. The abrupt shift from the calm upward movement of hammering, clipping and stepping to a sudden fall always shook Billy. He had fallen many times, with partners and alone. Years of aid climbing had taken their toll. With his scars and healed bones, Billy knew that a fall could leave him in serious pain. He tapped in a piton and clipped his webbing ladder to it. He rarely worried about his placements, but whenever he heard piton scratch against the rock, he would hold his breath and then calmly use his hammer to drive it farther into the crack.

Billy's canvas pants ripped when he dragged his legs over the pointy edges. "Look out below," Billy yelled when he trundled a large rock from a ledge. By mid-afternoon, he was exhausted from the manual labour. He smoked a joint and ate an orange. No one had climbed that high on the Goat Buttress before, but he was still far from the top, so he decided to rappel down. There were no cracks that could provide a safe place for a piton. The rock around the ledge he was perched on was frail and breaking away. Having spent so many hours of his life face to face with stone, he'd learned the subtleties of assessing how strong it was simply by looking at it or tapping it with his knuckle.

Billy started to drill a hole that he could hammer a small bolt into. He hummed his favourite Gordon Lightfoot song, "Canadian Railroad Trilogy." His only drill bit was dull from years of use. His first hole took 30 minutes to drill. Over Billy's shoulder to the east was Yamnuska. The peak had a dark cloud over it, like a floppy hat, that soon swirled down the face like a breaking wave. The same cloud system inched down the wall above Billy. He put on his black toque and doubled his sweaters. He was alone on the wall. He was hanging from small pieces of metal in a sea of grey rock. Three black ravens kept him company during his slow rappel. Pitch after pitch, Billy drilled bolt holes. Pitch after pitch, Billy was getting tired. His waist was swollen from the tight-woven harness straps, and his mouth was dry. He ate his last bit of food, a Mars bar, and smoked the roach in his pocket before his final rappel. He found a crack for a short piton, clipped in and tossed the rope. The sound of the rope falling meant it was time to trust his metallurgy, and once the end of the rope hit the ground, Billy went down. Blood from his wounded knuckles soaked into the cuffs of his brown sweater.

On the ground, he unclipped and dropped his gear. He was in the shadow of Goat Mountain, and it was starting to rain. He left his gear and made the trek back to the hut. Everything below his knees was saturated from melting snow. He arrived to a cold and quiet shelter containing warm clothes and food. He finished the whiskey and wrapped a wool blanket around himself. He rubbed his feet to warm his toes. His boots were gnarled from the rock and had many fresh holes. It was time to sleep, but Billy had something on his mind and he had to write it down.

Mar. 23, 1974:

The Bolting Trilogy (to be sung to The Railroad Trilogy by Gordon Lightfoot). By William Lighthead

There was a time in this fair land, when bolting was
    not done.
When the tall blank walls stood virgin in the sun.
Long before the Hardings and long before the steel.
When the tall blank walls were too silent to be real.

But time has no beginning and history has
    no bounds
And to these vivid walls they came from all around.
They drilled upon her blankness and put the routes
    up tall.
Put up the ladders and belays to the dismay of us all.

For they look into the future and what did they see.
They saw a bolt ladder running from the top to
    the screes.
Up blank walls to hanging belays.
Swinging their hammer and drawing dismay.

Look away said Robbins across these mighty walls
To Tis-sa-ack
I only used 110 in all, I only used 110 in all.

Behind the blue Rockies, the sun is declining.
The stars they are shining at the break of the day.
Across the wide walls the climbers lay stoned
In their hammocks in a land far away.

Oh, we are the bolters who work upon the walls
Swinging our hammers in the bright blazing sun.
Living on tuna and drinking bad water.
Putting in bolts, till the long day is done.

At noon the following day, Billy rolled out of his sleeping bag. There was new snow on the trees outside of the window. A foot of white powder blanketed the valley, hills and mountains. On the hut's shelf were a deck of cards, a jar of pens, a box of matches, two eight-track tapes, flagging tape, four unusable pitons and four partially readable books.

Billy grabbed the top book; it was Carlos Castaneda's *The Teachings of Don Juan: A Yaqui Way of Knowledge*. Castaneda claimed he had apprenticed under a Yaqui sorcerer named Don Juan. Popular among the counter-culture climbers in western Canada, the book elevated Mexican shamanism to the forefront of the hippie movement. Carlos recounted speaking to Mescalito, the teaching spirit that inhabits all peyote plants, and transforming into a blackbird after using the magic mushroom known as "humito," which means "little smoke." The Squamish Hardcore were inspired by the book to name their new routes on El Capitan Mescalito and Magic Mushroom. In Gordie Smaill's first Squamish guidebook, he referred to the cliffs in town as "Little Smoke Bluffs" — his clever way of calling them the "magic mushroom bluffs."

Billy flipped the paperback book open and started to read: "For me there is only the traveling on paths that have heart, on any path that may have heart, and the only worthwhile challenge is to traverse its full length — and there I travel looking, looking breathlessly." In the evening, Billy went outside and walked through deep snow up to the shoulder of Yamnuska to sit below Raven's End. Back in the hut, he wrote the following:

Yaa-man-wow — felt like somebody else — it doesn't
matter — o.k. — far out — fantastic — mainly vegetables — though this was supposed to — far out man
— steam-yam tastes good — Christ — is there more of
that left — tea Billy — thank you — sizzle-steam — ta
— good supper — far out — hungry — good — doesn't
take long time to cook spring vegetables — salt and
pepper good-mmm-good-mmm good-good — fire-
crackle-G-trees make good wood don't they? — wind-
burst burst burst — ahhha — crackle-stew-laugh-shoe
— cut my toe nails now — because it wasn't frost bit
— ooo my head owwww.

A week went by and the snow was melting, so Billy
retrieved his gear from Goat Buttress. He had lucked
out and caught a number of rabbits using a snare trap
that week. After skinning the rabbits, he hung the furs
outside the hut and cooked the meat in a pot. One night
after a successful hunt and big dinner, he wrote the following in the hut logbook:

> Seeing the snow and light through the trees today,
> with spectrums of diffused light. And one gliding.
> The wind of time blowing through your hair, I stop
> and wonder why I'm there.
>
> I felt what it is like to be a warrior, a person with
> oneself. To be at one with your surroundings, neither
> better than nor less than, but just as your surround-
> ings, nothing matters but everything matters you see
> things as they are and are enchanted. — This is really
> how it should be — Really.

*   *   *

Billy returned to Calgary a few days later. Sorting through his journals, he found the list of potential Yamnuska climbs that he had published in the 1970 CMC newsletter. All of the routes on the list had been climbed — all but one:

> Yellow Edge V A5 F9
>
> The prominent buttress bounding the Bowl on the right. Start by a corner, F8, and continue by a series of increasingly difficult corners to the right of the main buttress.

Yellow Edge was a 200-metre prow of grey and yellow limestone. The top of the feature overhung the base by 50 metres. For a climber, it was an obvious challenge. To its left and right were weaknesses that climbers had tried. The Yellow Edge was not the biggest route on Yamnuska, but it was the last clear line from the ground to the top that hadn't been climbed. Billy made plans to try it with Urs.

They left a few days later and parked in a spot where they had many times before. They carried their heavy packs back to the base of the Yellow Edge. Urs had never tried the route, but Billy was familiar with the first section of steep rock. After Billy climbed the first ratshit-infested corner, where rocks broke under his body weight, Urs took the lead. He pounded pitons into cracks and pulled on them. The rock was wildly overhanging, and the wind blew with intensity. Their clothes fluttered like laundry blowing in a gale. Billy hung off a nylon sling to belay Urs. Halfway up the pitch, Urs stopped at a challenging section and yelled to Billy how hard it was. Urs pushed his right knee against the prickly stone until the friction supported his weight. He pushed his back into the opposing side of the chimney. With his elbow pushing down, he squirmed upwards, grimacing. After some hard moves, each more painful than the last, Urs succeeded in reaching a ledge. He stopped to catch his breath. The Yellow Edge was proving to be a formidable challenge.

Billy climbed the rope using a prusik and stopped on a ledge where Urs was belaying. He lit a cigarette, sorted his gear and then led up the third pitch, following a corner above the belay. He stopped below a blank wall and drilled holes for small rivets. At a ledge, he hammered pitons in for a belay. Urs followed. They pulled whiskey and oranges out of their packs and decided to let their skin heal for the evening. As the temperature dropped, they pushed into each other to stay warm. Frost formed deep in the chimneys and cracks overnight.

In the morning, the silhouettes of Calgary's buildings could be seen to the east. Billy rolled a cigarette as the sun made its way above the prairies. They snacked on rye bread and shared a Mars bar. They packed their beds, and Billy climbed the fourth pitch. He started up a flaring corner that narrowed at the top to the width of his fingers. Billy then moved from a sloping ledge and started to build a bolt ladder up and right. He was far above the trees on an overwhelmingly exposed piece of rock. He drilled and hammered and drilled some more until he was past the bulge of steep rock. Urs climbed the rope. Billy had a lot of pitons left and unclipped them from his gear loop. He then clipped them on Urs's gear sling. *Clink, clink, clack,* and Urs was off.

The prow above was not climbable by Urs's standards, and he drifted right. He made some hard free climbing moves and then aided on tied-off knife blades; his right hand was bloody from the day's work. Banging iron into untravelled walls was done only by climbers burly enough to endure the pain and the time it took. He ended his pitch on a ledge 50 metres below the summit ridge. The two pitches took most of the day. Instead of climbing the rope, Billy stayed lower down for the night. He could see the Goat Buttress, Urs's car and the edge of Calgary under the night sky. He didn't know it yet, but this was the last night he would ever spend on Yamnuska.

At sunrise, Billy shed a few layers and climbed up the rope. Looking down past his leather boots, he could see the ground hundreds of feet below. He and Urs shared a brief word about which way to climb, and Billy started up. No climber had ever been here before. As with any new climb, finding the best way was like piecing together a puzzle. Could they reach the summit? Billy started to the right of Urs. He hammered some shallow-placed bolts until he reached a right-facing corner, where he banged in pitons. There was loose rock on the last few metres of the Yellow Edge. Billy yelled to Urs to watch out. The wind howled too loud for Urs to hear anything. Billy reached the top.

From there, Billy moved onto the north slope of Yamnuska. Urs followed up the pitch. To keep Urs safe while he climbed, Billy used what Urs called the "fingertip belay." They were soon safe on the climber's descent trail.

*   *   *

They returned to Calgary, but Billy made his way back to the hut a few days later. As the days passed, he fell into a routine: coffee and then a cigarette before packing for the day. Then he would go hunting at the base of Yamnuska and on the slopes around the hut. He always had something to eat for dinner. One night, he had three grouse. In June, other climbers started to arrive at the hut. They knew Billy and would sometimes bring him oranges, sardines or tobacco. The hut's location was hidden from hikers on Yamnuska and tucked into trees near the north valley. Climbers were always happy when they arrived to find that Billy had the wood stove going. But he also spent many days alone.

> Hi again,
>
> Today is the day after yesterday and the day before tomorrow. Now that we got our days straight, I've got something to tell you. Hey, wait, don't run away, please stay. Oh, won't you, please, then fuck off. Go away, come again some other day, oh hum. To be by one's self, but wait, I see trees blowing in the wind, grass like a restless sea, clouds billowing into all sorts of spiritual things and rocks gleaming in the sparkling threads of sun dew. And splashing bobbling liquid steam with shades of green, purple hues, blues and violet sheens. I'm not alone. Just now a squirrel scared the living shit out of me.

*   *   *

Just made a cup of rose hip tea. Oh, the wonders of nature. I overdosed on vitamin C.

*   *   *

Today is like all other days and I don't know the time. This is the fourth day — I think?

*   *   *

Had a joint and then began to fix the window. Far out. Look at this hole in the wall. Ah, what do you call it? Ah, they say one loses his mind on dope. That's absolutely propos, ah, what's the word, I forget, oh well, doesn't matter. I forgot what I was going to say anyway. He he he, ha ha ha, ho ho ho. Boy, is it ever windy out, or is it in, that's right, I'm on the roof. No, I'm in the bog. Well then, in that case, boy is it ever smelly around here. No, that's your armpits, did you say the rat shit? No, I said your farts did, far out.

On June 18, Jon Jones and George Homer visited Billy at the hut. The previous summer, George had seen a line on the west face of Frodo Buttress in the CMC Valley he wanted to climb. Billy was keen to join. Within a few hours, the trio climbed to the top of a rippled stone prow. The first pitch was the hardest, and the route eased the higher they climbed. Back in the hut, George cooked vegetable and rabbit stew. Billy sketched the route in the logbook and wrote down what they'd done.

June 19, 1974:

False Modesty 5.8+, 700 feet, Billy Davidson, Jon Jones, George Homer

Iron: nuts, two regular Lost Arrows.

Pitch one, 40 metres, 5.10a. Climb the crack (piton) to a belay in the bowl.

Pitch two, 30 metres, 5.8. Climb the wide crack on the left side of the bowl and continue to the top of a pinnacle.

Pitch three, 40 metres, 5.9. Move left from the pinnacle and climb a steep slab (piton) past a shattered block on the left to a corner and a second piton runner. Move up and make a difficult traverse left to easier ground. Continue up a groove to the ridge.

Pitches four to six, easy fifth-class climbing up the ridge leads to the top of the buttress.

In July, Billy went on three-day hunting trip for mountain goats. The large-horned animals roamed the ridgelines at the far end of the valley, often in groups of up to 15. Billy was rained on and didn't get any sleep. After a few days of hunting, he returned the hut empty handed. He then drew a cartoon of himself hunting and the animals hiding underground.

Back at the hut, Billy had a string of pan-sized trout and brewed pine needle tea. The lodgepole pines around the hut were knocking back and forth in a storm. Billy packed his Drum and hiked to the top of Yamnuska. He hadn't been to the summit for a few weeks. Alone on top of his favourite mountain, he watched the sun set below the western peaks before hiking back to the hut.

He went hunting two days later wearing a deer hide vest and leather bandana. A small hare hopped within two metres of his perch in the woods. He killed the rabbit on his first draw and cooked it for dinner. Shortly after that, he had the urge to free-solo a route on Yamnuska. After he climbed an easy 30 metres, it rained, and Billy climbed down the slippery stone. In the logbook, he wrote:

> July 5, 1974 (I think) Friday anyway
>
> Gone hunting below Yamnuska.
>
> Up, down and all around. Then we landed on the ground. Finally, we're homeward bound. The sky precipitates on our minds, with its arms of lead it binds, thereby preventing the climbs.

A few days later, Urs wanted to climb up the centre of Ha Ling Peak's north face. Billy was interested, as he had fond memories from his early climb there with John Braun. Billy and Urs hadn't seen each other since Yellow Edge. Approaching the 600-metre unclimbed north face of Ha Ling, Billy traced his hand along the path that he'd taken eight years before. He turned to Urs and said, "You know what, man, that wall looks too easy for aiding. Someone will free climb that someday, let's leave it for them."

Urs and Billy watched the clouds rise against east face of East End of Rundle and ate sandwiches that Gerda had made. Urs knew he would be back, and he was right — a decade later, he climbed a new route straight up the middle of the face with a South African climber named David Cheesmond. But not Billy. This was the last time he would stand beneath Ha Ling.

Chapter 13

BACK TO YOSEMITE

*I had mixed feelings upon getting to the top. I was glad
to have done the climb, and to have done it in three days.
Yet it had been such an incredible climb I was sad to see
it end. Who would not want to keep climbing at such
a high calibre, in such an incredible place, on a climb
with this much history and in such perfect weather?... It
was a significant achievement for us personally and for
Canadian climbing.*

—NEIL BENNETT, ON HIS FIRST CANADIAN
ASCENT, WITH GORDIE SMAILL, OF THE NOSE

THE GOLDEN LARCH TREES WARNED OF
winter, and after five months of living behind
Yamnuska, Billy moved back into his dad's house. The
dull wallpaper and drab carpet made Billy wish he was
back in the hut. He owed money to a bank for his motorbike and didn't have a job. He heard that John Lauchlan
and his wife, Judy, were in Yosemite, so Billy packed a
small bag of clothes, jumped on his Harley and headed
to California. He arrived in Camp 4 a few days later.

It was snowing in Canada when he left, but temperatures in Yosemite were nice for climbing. Billy later

told Urs how impressive he found the trees in the valley — trees like the ponderosa pine, a big evergreen with bark of irregularly shaped plates and dark furrows; the incense-cedar with its feathery, reddish bark; and the California black oak, with yellow-green leaves and a dark trunk. In Camp 4, the bigleaf maple's yellow leaves overlapped with the dark oranges on the black oaks and the reds and pinks of dogwoods and sugar maples.

A week before Billy made the trip, Calgary climbers Gary Jennings and Bruce Keller had driven Bruce's Pontiac Astra down. At the border, they were given a two-week visa, but they stayed in Yosemite for six. Billy told Gary he hadn't brought any climbing gear but was interested in doing a climb with him. Other climbers at the camp pitched in equipment. As the sun set on El Capitan and bonfires crackled, Billy and Gary made their plan of attack. Despite never having climbed together, they agreed to try a route up the biggest section of El Capitan. The next morning, John took a photo of a smiling Billy and a wide-eyed Gary.

Billy wanted to climb the Triple Direct, more or less the easiest route on El Cap. First climbed by Jim Bridwell and Kim Schmitz, it had most recently been climbed a year earlier by Beverly Johnson and Sibylle Hechtel, the first all-woman team up the wall. The Triple Direct takes the first ten pitches of the Salathé Wall and then continues up the middle portion of El Capitan via the Muir Wall and finishes on the upper pitches of the Nose. It climbs only one independent pitch but is considered an individual route because of its historical context. Most climbers would finish the route in a few days, but Billy wanted to do it in six. He called it vertical camping. They would bring Coors Banquet and a lot of food. The haul bags were old, beaten, torn up and held together with webbing. Gary had never nailed iron, so at the camp, Billy went over the finer points of the craft: "Bang, bang, ping and ping, then clip and high step." Gary got the idea. For food it would be military rations. Billy scored them a week's worth of corn, beef and peas. For treats, they had butter and rye crisp.

By eight a.m. they were ready, and John and Judy saw them off. Everyone else was out climbing. "Jimmy Page is the best and you know it," John said to Gary. "Not a chance, all Hendrix," Gary yelled back. With a campfire simmering, Billy and Gary walked off with oversized packs pulling their shoulders down. They made the quick approach to base of the 1000-metre wall. Billy tightened his bandana and clipped dozens of pitons to slings around his chest, retied his boots and started up. By Billy's numbers, they had to climb just under 200 metres a day.

The rock was cold to the touch. Between bashing pitons, Billy breathed hot air into his hands. At only 20 metres off the frosty grass, Billy stopped to warm and put on his down coat. One knuckle was already bloody, but he carried on, leaving a trace of blood on the stone for Gary to follow. After ten hours of nailing, they were on the Triangle ledges, safely clipped to bolts and hauling the gear. No beers were cracked until the bashing was done. Gary opened one for Billy first, then they toasted a good day. Below, John, Judy and George Homer hollered up about how warm the fire was. Billy and Gary sank into their sleeping bags, happy to be off the valley floor.

That's how the next few days went. Nailing, bashing, hauling, scraping, pulling and pushing, free climbing, sleeping, bleeding, cursing, hollering and eating. Climbing higher and higher, they noticed George Homer and a partner nailing up the Nose. Where Billy and Gary's route joined the Nose was called the Crossroads, a small ledge big enough for two. From there, they saw George far below. That night, after a few beers, Billy and Gary started to throw beer cans down onto the lower climbers. Under the starry sky, George yelled profanities, answered by laughs and howls from Billy and Gary — and soon Gary was laughing uproariously with them. It went like that until the cold forced everyone into their nests. There was no wind that night, and the folks in the valley could hear the climbers snoring.

Billy awoke in the middle of the night to pee. It was a tiresome act that required more messing around than he wished for. Standing on the edge of Camp IV (not to be confused with Camp 4 in the valley — the ledges where climbers sleep are given Roman numerals up to VI), he lit a cigarette. In the morning, Gary had to poo. When climbers had to relieve themselves, liquids went over the side and solids went anywhere, usually into cracks in the rock. In 1974, that wasn't an issue. In later years, crap on climbs became a problem. Gary told Billy to look away as he added to the growing compost.

That morning, Billy and Gary took it easy and only climbed a short distance to Camp IV, about 50 metres. They wasted the day getting wasted. That night, the sling from Gary's hammer that wrapped around his chest levered his cigarette pack out of his shallow breast pocket. The smokes fell into the Camp IV shitting crack, which was the width of a man's arm and a metre long. Gary wasn't going to go in after the smokes; Billy was hoping he'd make an effort for the campfire story. On the wall, when your smokes are gone, your smokes are gone. Gary didn't expect any sympathy from Billy — after all, he was the rookie. Billy offered him a few cigarettes, and they shared a gut-stitching laugh.

Billy took his wool hat and sweater off and clipped the heavy pitons to his sling. They were three days from the top of El Capitan. For 700 metres, the wall swooped below them to a point at the base of the Nose. "You know, Gary, life is like a ladder," said Billy. "Most people start at the bottom rung and climb up from there. But to me, life is like an escalator; I get on at the bottom and it carries me up. Even if I take a step back, I still keep on going up." Gary, unsure what to think, didn't say anything.

Up Billy went. The air carried the rings of his hammer across the valley. Tourists below who had come for the fall colours were transfixed by the action on the rock above and watched with binoculars. John and Judy watched too.

It was all perfection to Billy, and he was happy to be up there. He hammered his way towards Camp V and then took the next pitch, the most classic pitch on El Cap, the Great Roof. After a few free moves from Dolt Tower, he started to hammer. The going was easy. The exposure below was mind-boggling. Billy was aiming for a thin crack up and right. Far out from the belay, he looked down between his legs, hundreds of metres straight to the ground. At the far end, he paused to look back at what he'd climbed. Billy often talked about what Carlos Castaneda had said, and might have been thinking it then: "Only as a warrior can one withstand the path of knowledge. A warrior cannot complain or regret anything. His life is an endless challenge, and challenges cannot possibly be good or bad. Challenges are simply, challenges."

Once he was above the roof, the climbing eased into the Pancake Flake. A few hours later, Billy and Gary were hanging at Camp V. Once they were settled for the night, Billy cracked a beer and closed his eyes. He thought about the first ascent of the Nose while Gary enjoyed rye crisps. They communicated to the ground crew by throwing cans containing messages (the story went that, on occasion, love letters had been tossed from Dolt Tower and Camp IV in a Hunt's tomato can).

At Camp V, there were ledges named Warren's bedroom, Wayne's bedroom and the sun deck. Warren's was the large middle one. Wayne's was the small one down below, with its anchor way up above on Warren's bedroom, so there was strong incentive not to roll over — or even sleep, for that matter. The sun deck was the highest one. Billy was sleeping in Warren's bedroom and Gary in Wayne's. The great Gaston Rébuffat once said:

> Some mountaineers are proud of having done all their climbs without bivouac. How much they have missed! And the same applies to those who enjoy only rock climbing, or only the ice climbs, only the ridges or faces. We should refuse none of the thousand and one joys that the mountains offer us at every turn. We should brush nothing aside, set no restrictions. We should experience hunger and thirst, be able to go fast, but also to go slowly and to contemplate.

In the morning, Gary took the lead up a left-facing corner to the gloomy Glowering Spot, a frowning rock alcove. They then climbed to Camp VI, the final camp. It was a small two-person triangular ledge, the top of a pillar. They had ten beers left and drank them all. George was at Camp V, close enough to communicate with. It was their sixth night on the wall, and the coldest. After a few beers, hundreds of metres above the forest, Gary started to sing Jimi Hendrix's "Purple Haze." Billy played air guitar and shouted good night to George.

They started earlier than normal the following morning because they were out of smokes, beers and weed and wanted off the wall. Gary led, then Billy, and then Gary to the Wild Stance. From there, he held his camera out and pointed it down to Billy, who was holding onto the etriers and smiling. Behind him was a sheer grey wall that dramatically dropped to the bottom tip of the Nose. The picture would become one of Gary's favourites. Billy led up an easy bolt ladder and then Gary ran up easy terrain, which left Billy to take it to the summit. As Billy climbed the last pitch, he thought about the words of Warren Harding: "As I hammered in the last bolt and staggered over the rim, it was not at all clear to me who the conqueror was and who was the conquered. I do recall that El Cap seemed to be in much better condition than I was."

To Billy's surprise, John and Judy were waiting for them on top. Billy hugged everyone and started to pull the rope up. He had on a heavy grey wool sweater and black pants, with an orange belt made from webbing and an orange bandana. John and Judy had on baggy wool sweaters, and John was wearing his thick-framed glasses and a turtleneck under his sweater. It was cloudy as Gary topped out in his very baggy beige wool sweater. His pants were torn wide open. He and John looked like brothers with their shoulder-length wavy hair and glasses. Not Billy — he looked like a young Warren Harding. They hiked off El Capitan in daylight, and by nightfall they were at the valley bar. Almost all the Canadians in camp were there — it was a big Canadian party. They yelled up to George, who was likely asleep.

The next day, John, Gary and Billy hitched out of the valley to the nearest place they could rent pedal bikes, and then took some mescaline. Billy, wearing his favourite dashiki and denim bell-bottoms, marvelled at the altered sense of time and self, the brilliant and intense colours, the recurring patterns. The trip reached its climax when a lightning storm lit the valley walls and thunder shook the trees.

*   *   *

A few days later, Billy rode his Harley back to his dad's house in Calgary. After a few days visiting, he packed a bag for a weekend at the Archie Simpson hut and walked out the front door of the house. To his surprise, his Harley was missing. Billy's uninsured motorbike had been stolen. He phoned his friends, but no one had seen it. Urs told Billy the culprit was probably the bikers who sold it to him; it was a common scam to sell bikes and then steal them back.

The following day, Billy wrote a letter to his dad: "Dear dad, I'm going west to meet my friend Rob. See you soon." He didn't tell anyone else that he was leaving Alberta. His thumb wasn't up for too long before a pickup truck driving to Revelstoke stopped. From there, Billy caught a ride with a semi-truck driver to the coast. The air was muggier farther west, as a high-pressure system from California had just arrived. The truck parked beneath a half-moon that lit the mountains on the eastern edge of the Fraser Valley. Walter Bonatti once said that a great alpinist can sleep anywhere, even in a ditch. More than once, Billy found himself sleeping where he didn't expect.

Chapter 14

THE PACIFIC NORTHWEST

*We had to pass over huge rocks... I have been for a long
period among the Rocky Mountains, but have never seen
any thing like this country. It is so wild that I cannot find
words to describe our situation at times. We had to pass
where no human being should venture; yet in those places
there is a regular footpath impressed, or rather indented
upon the very rocks by frequent travelling.*

—*SIMON FRASER*

THE INSIDE PASSAGE, WHERE ALASKA, BRITISH
Columbia and Washington State meet the Pacific
Ocean, is a 1600-kilometre chain of island archipel-
agos that remain mostly unvisited. It has over 50,000
kilometres of coastline. Big Pacific Ocean swells break
on the western shores, but the waters of the Inside
Passage are protected, calm, complex and shrouded
in mystery. Much of it is too perilous to visit. Never-
before-climbed mountains are draped in cascading
waterfalls. Untouched glaciers exist at higher eleva-
tions. The Coast Mountains stretch 1600 kilometres
down the coast to Fraser River and run 200 kilometres
towards the interior. Along the coast, a number of

First Nations groups have claims to land, including Gwa'sala-'Nakwaxda'xw, Wuikinuxv, Heiltsuk, Nuxalk, Haisla and Tsimshian.

The thousands of islands along the continent's edge have a rich diversity of marine life, including whales, sea lions, dolphins, salmon and sharks. The coastal rainforest is home to otters, wolves, deer, grizzly and brown bears, the spirit bear and seabirds. Mosquitoes thrive in windless and shady areas. Blackflies are bad near estuaries when it's hot. Sand flies often swarm kayaks on the water and are bad on beaches on warm days. The wet and mild climate allows the western hemlocks, Douglas firs, Amabilis firs, lodgepole pines, vine maples, yellow cedar, red alder, Sitka spruce, black cottonwoods, red alders and bigleaf maples to grow to massive sizes. Below the trees is the shrub layer, made up of red huckleberry, salal, Alaska blueberry and Oregon beaked moss. Life is dictated by the currents, inflow and outflow winds and the two basic tide types: spring tides (strongest) and neap tides (weakest). Each tide peaks about 24 times a year.

The Inside Passage was in its natural state in the 1970s. A few kayakers had visited the area over the years preceding Billy's first visit, finding isolated beaches with driftwood that could be used for firewood and building. Some camps were close to freshwater, sheltered and unaffected by tides; some camps were above high-backed beaches that remained somewhat exposed at spring tides. The size of beach sediment — pebbles, rocks, cobble and grit — changed from place to place. Clamshell beaches, usually found on small islets, were the best for camping, with no sediment to track around and not many insects.

When Billy arrived in Vancouver, he went in search of Rob Wood on Granville Island, a 40-acre man-made island built in 1917 by the Canadian Pacific Railway. Thanks to a letter Rob had sent Billy earlier that year, which included a sketch of the location, Billy knew he could find him living in a renovated industrial building called Clay's Wharf. Seagulls squawked as hundreds of sailboats bobbed and banged off piers. Waves lapped on sterns and tugboats putted in and out of the channel. Along the boardwalk, low tide exposed the pier's bar-nacle-covered beams. The high-pressure system was coming to an end. On the horizon, over swaying trees, dark cloud approached. Standing at the pier's edge, Billy watched the smoke from his cigarette blow into the oncoming storm. Between gusts of wind, he heard a familiar British accent. It was Rob, yelling down from the rickety second level.

After moving to the west coast, Rob had bought a sailboat from some folks he met at Clay's — he had always wanted to sail to less-travelled mountains to make first ascents. He named it *Shadowfax*, after Gandalf's horse in *The Lord of the Rings*, who "carried him to safety in disaster's way." The warm late-summer weather meant there was little snow on the high peaks of the Coast Mountains. Billy and Rob came up with a plan to sail north along the coast to climb Mount Waddington.

It was to be Billy's maiden voyage. Rob had some marine training from sea cadets in high school and experience from short day trips in *Shadowfax*. Neither of them knew how to find Waddington. Looking at the few charts they had, Rob figured that Bute Inlet would be their best bet. Billy didn't question this, and after packing smokes, fishing rods and a few other essentials, they were set.

Shadowfax was hitched by stern, bow and spring lines to metal cleats on the dock. The white haul and strong-looking mast grabbed Billy's attention. The cabin smelled of damp cedar, and the boat came equipped with life jackets, lanterns, bottle openers and books.

Billy unhitched the boat and they were off. Rob nervously steered the vessel between anchored sailboats and buoys. They had climbed some of the biggest vertical rock walls in America, but the flat water ahead of them was a new adventure.

The hazards on a rock climb were different than on the ocean. A successful climber had to be aware of overhead hazards such as rock and ice. But on the ocean, Billy and Rob had to concern themselves with currents, tides and fixed objects. The tidal rapids could move up to 15 knots and produced dangerous whirlpools. There wasn't much fuel on board, which could be a problem if there was no wind or too much fog. Fishermen at the wharf warned Rob about rocks beneath the surface that could tear the keel off.

Unaccustomed to the sudden motions of *Shadowfax*, both Billy and Rob got seasick. Sailing north up the open strait near the coastal town of Powell River, *Shadowfax* galloped towards Desolation Sound. A strong southeast wind picked up, and they struggled to stay on course. Billy was sat high on the deck with salt water splashing on him; his Lee jeans were soaked through. Rob manned the tiller, outfitted in the only rubber coat on board. The tiller was maxed, but *Shadowfax* continued windward into the waves. Despite their inexperience, they managed to reduce the main sail and overcome the first crux of their voyage. Billy lit a smoke and fished for whatever he could catch.

At nightfall, Rob slowed the boat as Billy probed the depth of the water. Rob nosed *Shadowfax* into the mouth of a river. They were looking for water sheltered from big waves but still deep enough for the keel at low tide. They decided five metres was good. But on some subsequent nights, Rob would just say, "The piss with it, toss the anchor, let's sleep." Their luck held: they never bottomed out Shadowfax.

Bute Inlet proved too much of an undertaking, and after passing East Redonda on its eastern shore, Billy and Rob found their way into Toba Inlet, 20 kilometres south of Bute. Snow-capped peaks rose 3000 metres out of the ocean. Steep granite walls dressed with thick forests stood around Billy and Rob in every direction. It was total isolation on pristine waters. A sea otter circled the boat.

Billy sat with Rob on the deck, flipping through a book on coastal plants. "It's an arbutus," he said, pointing out a broadleaf tree with a crooked trunk, twisting branches and rounded crown. Rob was busy coiling ropes and learning new knots from a book of his own. "Aha, bowline on a bite," he said. Billy pointed at a shrub with slender limbs. "A Douglas maple, that one there." Out of the corner of his eye, above the splashing otter, he spotted a western red cedar. Billy passed out on the bow and Rob at the helm.

In the morning, they took the raft to shore and, with no climbing gear, aimed to hike the mountain closest to them. There was no trail, and the terrain was steep and rugged, the coastal brush hard to bushwhack, dense with stinging devil's club, obstructing slide alder and swarming mosquitoes. After hours of battling, Billy and Rob came to a small meadow with an alpine lake. Even in the fall, the still water bred countless mosquitoes. Billy and Rob couldn't defend themselves and simply moved with the clouds of bloodsucking bugs. There were no mosquitoes like this in the Rockies. From the top of the likely unclimbed peak, they looked out upon countless mountains and unvisited islands.

Sailing back through the Discovery Islands archipelago, Rob took note of the beauty. Billy felt they were leaving too soon; they had so much exploring to do. But Rob was drawn back to Clay's Wharf, which he knew was the cheapest place to moor *Shadowfax*. As they drifted towards the dock, a woman nursing a baby greeted them. Soon they were having drinks with folks Rob had never met, discussing the City's plan to evict people from Clay's Wharf as part of the Granville Island redevelopment. The room smelled of incense and patchouli. Billy left to finish cleaning *Shadowfax*, but Rob, who had a Ph.D. in progressive alternative communities, stayed in the room. Rob was asked if he would like to buy a quarter section of land on Maurelle Island in the northern Georgia Strait. He wasn't sure about the deal because he hadn't seen the land. Later, though, Rob learned that Maurelle was part of the Discovery archipelago, which he had fallen so in love with on his trip with Billy. The deal was for ten people to pay $3,000 each for whatever piece of land they wanted on the 15-square-kilometre island. Rob bought into the plan and moved to Maurelle.

That same winter, he frequently visited Squamish to connect with the Squamish Hardcore. One night at the Chieftain Hotel, he met a climber named Laurie Mason.

"Apart from her other attributes, I figured (quite rightly, as it turned out) that any girl who could climb so well could do pretty well anything she put her mind to," Rob told me. "To the permanent chagrin of the Hardcore, I persuaded her to join me on the island retreat, along with her four-year-old daughter, Kiersten. Together we built a homestead, where we married and live happily."

Billy did the opposite and found reclusion on the beaches of Vancouver. He wintered on the North Shore and later disappeared into the woods around Squamish. He had met a girl from Powell River named Dianne Logan, and he told her he wanted to return to Calgary for some rock climbing. That summer, they packed Dianne's big Ford pickup truck with salmon and headed west. It was like old times at the Empress. Friends bought Billy beers in honour of his Triple Direct climb.

With Urs and Rob Mitchell, Billy approached a new climb on Goat Mountain. Urs brought the gear and rope and packed a few sandwiches. Billy spotted a line of weakness and started up. A few months on the west coast hadn't shaken his nerve. He banged in bolts and hung off sky hooks. It started to rain, so Urs and Rob built a shelter using sticks and plastic.

Back on the ground, they sat shoulder to shoulder. It was cold out. The orange fixed rope flipped around in the wind. They made a fire that roared in the gusts. Billy's hair was long, the tips lightened from his time on the Pacific. He wore a thick, insulated coat and wool sweater. They posed for a timed photo. Urs wore a pointy toque, Norwegian ski sweater, and a thin down vest with big boots. Rob Mitchell was a small-framed man who would soon move to South America. Like Urs, he wore a wool sweater and vest for their climb.

With the westerly wind came snow; it was too cold to finish the route they were attempting. Once the sun rose, they cleaned their gear and walked back in the ankle-deep snow to Urs's van. Billy wrote in his journal:

> I looked back along the base of Yamnuska. How many times had I been along there? How many times had all of us been out to climb old Yam? It was without a doubt the CMC's stomping ground, their playground. If only Yam could talk, what a tale it would tell — the countless epics; sweat, blood; the noisy passage of this boorish lot.

Chapter 15

AYAK

Consider the subtleness of the sea; how its most dreaded creatures glide under water, unapparent for the most part, and treacherously hidden beneath the loveliest tints of azure... Consider all this; and then turn to this green, gentle, and most docile earth; consider them both, the sea and the land; and do you not find a strange analogy to something in yourself?

—HERMAN MELVILLE

BILLY MADE HIS WAY BACK TO VANCOUVER, where he stayed with some friends, one of whom lent Billy a book on kayaking. Billy had paddled small boats when he was at Wood's Home, but he had never used a long kayak with hatches designed for the ocean. The book's first chapter was about how to paddle, and the next was about great voyages. In 1928, a man named Franz Romer crossed the Atlantic Ocean over 58 days, but later died in a hurricane. Then, in 1932, Oskar Speck began his paddle from Germany to Australia, which ended in 1939, one year after Heinrich Harrer, Fritz Kasparek, Anderl Heckmair and Wiggerl Vörg made the first ascent of the classic north face of the Eiger in in Switzerland. Hannes Lindemann sailed his boat *Aerius II* from the Canary Islands to the Caribbean in 1956 and wrote about it in *Alone at Sea*.

Kayaks had at least a 5,000-year history on Canada's west coast by the time Billy arrived. At least 40 different designs have been documented in Canada, Alaska, Greenland and Siberia. Each design had a purpose, with some for hunting seals and whales and others for cruising rivers and chasing caribous. In the 1960s, 17-year-old George Dyson discovered his passion for kayaking after a trip to Alaska. He made a modern-day replica of an ancient kayak using nylon and aluminum. Within a few months, he and three friends had founded the first composite kayak company in western Canada. The Frontiersman fibreglass kayak was patented in 1976 and sold out of Mission, BC.

It was around then that Billy found himself a Frontiersman kayak, which he called *Ayak*, after the Iñupiaq word for a whaling harpoon. He also bought a seven-foot kayaking paddle. Billy was one of the first paddlers on Canada's west coast to own a fibreglass boat. He packed his few belongings into the front of the two-person kayak and rigged a small mast to help him move faster in the right winds.

His plan was to paddle off, solo, with no experience. He didn't know what he would eat or where he would sleep, but he did know that the most significant influence on his day-to-day activity would be the tides. During a full moon, the big tides brought spawning herring and eulachon fish to the rivers. There were two high tides and two low tides each day. The highest was called the "high high" and the lowest the "low low." "At low tide the table is set," a fisherman once told Rob. He meant that you could dig for clams and find mussels, crabs, barnacles and abalone.

When the lowest of the low tides stood still, it was called "low water slack." The low water slack during the big moon tide was the best time to fish for cod and salmon. The flood tides at full moon dictated the lives of those who depended on the ocean. Billy heard rumours that when big tides and high-pressure systems hit a northwest wind, the birds, fish and trees would become hyperactive and the waves would peak high above the shoreline.

Billy pushed off from a dock near Nanaimo Harbour where a plank of wood was engraved, "It is never too late to be wise," a quote from Daniel Defoe's *Robinson Crusoe*. Surprised by the rising waves and the disappearing horizon beyond the crest, Billy paddled along the shoreline north until he found a place to camp. Injury could mean death. When he lived at the Archie Simpson hut, help was but a yell or limp away, but on the remote rugged coast, there would never be help. There was no sign-in book at the trailhead. To live off the land, to really live off the land, Billy would have to be meticulous with his routine and frugal like never before. He soon discovered that beaching *Ayak* at low low tide meant he would have to pull his boat to higher ground. Beaching at high tide was ideal.

Billy made his way to Rob Wood on the Maurelle Island commune. Visitors without boats couldn't reach the island by car; they had to drive to Campbell River and then take a ferry to Quadra Island, where Rob would pick them up in his small tin boat. Billy paddled through the rapids of Surge Narrows and found a beach on Maurelle where he shored *Ayak*. Up an abandoned forestry road, he found fresh-cut trees and bushes. Beyond that, a dozen young families, including Rob's, were clearing land and building homes. The island was subdivided into lots that the owners could do with as they wished. Rob and his family had lived on *Shadowfax* for a month until they chose a piece of land to build on: two acres of slash clearing overlooking the ocean. They used fir poles and cedar siding to make a shack. The windows were plastic, and for insulation they used egg cartons.

Billy arrived in time for the completion of the Cosmic Cabin, a small building behind Rob's homestead. Eagles, robins, woodpeckers, ravens, jays and even humming-birds could be spotted during most months of the year. Billy passed time by sitting on the edge of the clearing and watching the tidal currents swirl in changing light. Rob's neighbours would often visit for dinner. Some of them came from wealthy backgrounds; some had always led a hermit lifestyle. There would be alcohol, weed and acid. Rob and Laurie conducted "pagan" ceremonies that would sometimes last for days, with dancing and celebration. On winter solstice, Rob would light a fire that burned for seven days. It could be seen offshore by people in boats who braved the winter waters. The dark days on the island were psychologically taxing, but the Cosmic Cabin was warm and comfortable.

Billy stayed until the spring before leaving for new adventures in *Ayak*. He'd heard the Queen Charlotte Strait was the gateway to the Broughton Archipelago, which had less boat traffic than the waters between Campbell River and Howe Sound. On the morning of Billy's departure, he and Rob had coffee and eggs before he pushed off. He paddled north up the Johnstone Strait to the western tip of West Cracroft Island. From there, he paddled northeast to Turnour Island and eventually to Village Island. People on the water were friendly, and Billy always said hello to those he paddled past.

On Village Island, Billy met a number of Kwakwa̱ka̱'wakw people from the Mamalilikulla First Nation, whose main village is 'Mimkwa̱mlis, which means "village with rocks and island out front." Billy stayed for a few weeks and learned about eulachon, a small fish that the locals had been hunting for decades; its oil was calorie-rich and had many uses. As Rob would later recall:

> This foul-smelling concoction, [Billy] claimed, was especially helpful in combating the cold coastal damp. One time, he paddled his kayak up to the top of Knight Inlet to score some grease from the Natives. He was hoping to make a trade for some berry leather he had made and was giving his sales pitch explaining how it would provide all the vitamins they needed for winter. The old Indian looked at him and smiled. "Why don't you just make wine?" he asked. "Then you get your vitamins and you get pissed as well."

Billy eventually acquired a .22 shotgun and learned to hunt for seals. The first seal he ever shot sank to the ocean floor, which surprised him; he thought it would float. He jumped in and swam down to retrieve it. Billy described his experiences harvesting eulachon in a letter to Rob:

It was just madness!! There I was; just scooping up handfuls of Ooleegins [eulachon] and throwing them into my "big" s.s. pot. This was my 400th pound I was working on and I had just recently discarded my homemade drip-net due to Ooleegins getting gill-netted, making for a lengthy pick-out time. The Ooleegins were running so thick up each side of the river due to tidal drop. I'd stagger up the beach to my camp where I'd dump them on a tarp I had stretched on the ground. After 500 pounds I was getting a little pooped. Then I had this flash. I took *Ayak* down to the water's edge and proceeded to fill it with 600 more pounds, then I just left the kayak and ran a rope up to above high-water line.

My pit was ten feet square and about one foot deep with packed dirt bottom. The sides are lined with split cedar boards but the bottom is left so when the fish are dumped in the blood will drain into the earth. When all was finally dumped into the pit, there was some 1,250 pounds of Ooleegins. Now the pit would sit 10 to 15 days depending on the weather (the cooler, the longer the sitting time) before the cooking stage.

Next day, I got another 600 Ooleegins and strung them up above my fire to smoke/dry. The males are best for smoke/drying because they're not as oily as the females. Generally, the females run up first and are caught for the pit; then the males follow and are caught for smoke/drying.

Two days into his eulachon harvest, Billy noticed a dead seal outside a house. The residents told him they planned to use only the meat, for food. Billy asked if he could take the skin.

> They said sure, as long as I skinned it, so I did and from the skin made this far-out rain hat. (The seal was too small to make a rain jacket) All stitching is done with seal skin strips and the hat is very light and very water proof. To prepare the skin, I stretched it over a piece of plywood and left it to dry in the sun (not over a fire) for a few days. Then scraped off all fat, etc. Then it is ready for use. They also gave me some of the blubber and meat. The meat I roasted. Delicious! The blubber I made into oil but cutting into small pieces and putting that in my s.s. pot and that hung over the fire so it got only a little heat. I got a good quart of oil which I used to eat and put on my tools and leather goods. The stuff is really good.
>
> So, bye for now my beautiful friends and I hope everything works out on each of your ends (hahahahhahaha).

From time to time, Billy returned to Rob's, but most of the year he spent exploring the Broughton Archipelago. On one trip north from Rob's up Johnstone Strait, he paddled *Ayak* east, with the northwest winds howling down the Queen Charlotte Strait. It was a flow tide, so the water moved into shore. He checked his charts a fourth and fifth time. He avoided the rip off Donegal Head and headed south to Stubbs Island and up through Blackfish Sound to Swanson, where he made camp.

For the next week, he waited for the strong winds to pass, then packed *Ayak* to tour around the area, paddling around Green Rock alongside harlequin ducks before beaching in Carrie Bay. He paddled into the heart of the Broughton Archipelago and stopped at G̱wayasdums Village on Gilford Island. The small community, situated between Knight and Kingcome Inlets, is the traditional home of the Kwikwasut'inuxw people, who belong to the collective Qui'kwasi ki la or "living inside the mountains." Other groups in the collective include the Gwawa'enuxw, the Haxwa'mis and the Dzawada'enuxw, who shared eulachon rights in the Kingcome River. G̱wayasdums was a winter village for all four groups. For the next few weeks, Billy lived on Gilford Island.

Writing again to Rob, Billy shared more of the knowledge he had acquired:

> I have learned all sorts of neat things from the locals (one old guy in particular):
>
> A) For an egg substitute when you need wild flours to hold together better, etc. Use insides of sea urchins. They have sacs which resemble eggs, ½ cup beaten into a foam will work just like eggs. It can be dried for the winter and can be eaten raw spread on crackers, etc. (Neat, hey?)
>
> B) How to catch a sea-gull without a gun. Get some fishing line and a baited hook (clam, etc.) and set on a rock where they come to feed. Play out line to a suitable hiding spot. When the gull takes the clam, he will get hooked and will start to fly away. Just reel him in. (That's what's called fly fishing?) Smoked gull is supposed to be really good, too.

C) Oil from ratfish liver is good for tools, etc. Good for people troubled with arthritis. (Just rub oil on affected joints) To render oil from liver just place in glass jar and set in sunlight for a few days. Pour off oil into another container as it accumulates.

I also am making a crab trap because my bay is crawling with them. Imagine crab and huckleberry leather — mmmmmm.

Well, I got to get going and have some supper. I'm having a wild fruit salad, raw young tips of bladderwrack seaweed, raw seaside plantain, raw broadleaf plantain, raw giant vetch sprout and the young peas and pods, salal berries, huckleberries and broken up pieces of smoked/dried cod with oil poured over all. With this also eight chapatis with oil on them. Mmmm good!

So, take care everyone. Keep healthy and high.

Chapter 16

WESTERLY WINDS

Yes, we had made an excursion into another world and we
had come back, but we had brought the joy of life and of
humanity back with us. In the rush and whirl of everyday
things, we so often live alongside one another without
making any mutual contact. We had learned... that men
are good, and the earth on which we were born is good.
—HEINRICH HARRER

BILLY LEFT VANCOUVER IN THE SUMMER OF
1979 to visit Calgary. Brian Greenwood had sold his
Elbow Park mansion and moved to the west coast;
the golden era of the CMC was over. Instead of the
Empress, the club now met on Wednesdays at the Cecil,
a notoriously dangerous place. There were over 100
members, and the get-togethers evolved from sitting
around drinking beers to late-night dance parties. Urs
was the president and Chic Scott the vice. The club held
an annual hockey game called "The Canucks vs. The
Rest of the World." A number of Billy's friends had died
over the years, including Lloyd MacKay from cancer
and Bugs McKeith from a fall on Mount Assiniboine.
Eckhard Grassman had died with Gary Pilkington on

the north face of Edith Cavell. The many new members included Barry Blanchard, Geoff Powter and Kevin Doyle, who were focused on climbing big and difficult alpine routes around the world.

Billy and Urs wasted no time in making their way to Yamnuska. They hiked to the base of Red Shirt, where they had hiked hundreds of times before. Billy slung his hammer over his shoulder and racked a few pitons. He wasn't wearing a shirt when he started up. Forced into a corner of rock, his shaggy beard dragged along the prickly stone. At the top of the first pitch, he told Urs that he didn't want to go any farther. They went back down. It was the last time Billy would ever go climbing.

The two old friends went to the Cecil for beers. Urs told Billy that John Lauchlan and Bruce Keller had climbed a hard route in CMC Valley called the Maker. If either climber had fallen, they would have been badly injured. John had also made the first solo ascent of Takakkaw Falls in only two and a half hours, and had joined Jim Elzinga for a cold ascent of the north face of Mount Kitchener. They spent three midwinter days in -40°C temperatures and nearly died on the route. Nearly a decade after that, in 1982, John would die alone on the ice climb called Polar Circus. It was Jim and some other climbers who'd find John's body. An avalanche had swept him over a steep section of ice.

Joined by other climbers, Billy and Urs stayed at the Cecil until one a.m. and then made their way home. A few minutes after they left, a disgruntled employee pulled out a gun and killed two of the other employees. In the morning, Billy visited Urs and Gerda and told them how disgusted he was with how bad Calgary had become. He packed his bag and left for the coast. He never returned to Calgary or the Rockies.

Perry Davis, Billy's friend from Wood's, later said:

> By the time he moved to the coast, Billy was more of a hippie then a climber. It was time for him to say goodbye to Calgary, and to the mountains. He had proved he was as good as the best on Tis-sa-ack. He had shown himself and others that he had aid and techno-mechanical climbing all figured out. His interests turned to the next thing, and the next thing was living off the land. Living off the land appealed to another side of Billy. There was hardly anyone to tell him what to do, and he didn't need money — well, hardly any. He would sometimes send letters to his friends in Alberta. But over the years, he gradually slipped away from everyone he knew in Alberta. His family included.

*   *   *

Billy made his way to Rob Wood's, where he stayed through Christmas before paddling north to Knight Inlet. "There are thousand-foot granite walls falling straight in the inlet," he would later write to Urs. "The inlet is 50 miles long and it took me three days to paddle up to the head. What a wild place!"

Billy paddled north past Wyatt Bay and Bentley Rock, then west past Sonora and Discovery Mountain. He went past Blind Channel in the Johnstone Strait and west along the shore of Vancouver Island towards the village of Sayward. Some spots were easy to paddle and offered rest, and other places presented dangerous challenges. Spits and islets offered easy access to sheltered camp sites.

The big peaks of Newcastle Ridge, part of the Insular Mountains, caught Billy's eye. He continued to Telegraph Cove and north to Donegal Head on Malcolm Island. He paddled past a pod of orcas to Waddington Bay on Bonwick Island because he knew it was a good place to stop during the northwest winds. A flat light from overcast skies revealed a place to camp. At the head of the bay was a white beach and a view of the Fox Group islands. Rocks by the beach were covered with beaked moss, and a Sitka spruce stood nearby. That night, Billy dined on wild berries. In the morning, he paddled towards the Fox Group and found the protected Solitary Islet to the east. To the north were Mars, Tracey and Innis islands.

He slept on the eastern tip of Mars Island, where seals often lay. He collected driftwood for a makeshift bench. As the tide ebbed away from the rocks, Billy carried a bucket to collect clams, taking care not to slip — the rocks were covered in olive bladderwrack and sea lettuce, and one slip could have dire consequences. He found a pool of urchins and put them in his bucket to split at the fire. He gathered littleneck clams, and with his full bucket and extra salt water to keep everything fresh, he cautiously made his way up the beach. He lit a fire and cooked the meat; there was plenty, so he saved some for breakfast.

Later, after moving to a camp on Eden Island, he ran out of the few supplies he needed, so he built a camp that he could duplicate anywhere with very few supplies. His driftwood bed was raised one metre off the ground, with room underneath for his belongings. He arranged rope, carabiners and tarps so that one cord controlled his entire adjustable canopy. His fire pit had a three-tier rack system, one for cooking, one for warming and one for drying clothes. Other details would be refined over the years.

Timing his trips with the tides, Billy used his charts to navigate Cramer Passage to Evans Point, across from Echo Bay. A man named Stubby Schultz had once owned resource rights to the island. One winter's day, Stubby waved to his friends, walked into the woods and disappeared without a trace. Some people said he ran through the trees and jumped into the Pacific; others said he was still out there.

When the tide was right, he started his short paddle across the passage to the small settlement at Echo Bay. The sea had a thick foam floating on it. He passed old clam gardens — beaches modified with artificial tidal barriers to create hospitable environments for different species of clams to grow. Some of the gardens dated back thousands of years; the walls were up to two metres high and spanned kilometres.

Echo Bay was named for the echoes that bounced off of a 100-metre wall to its north. Billy pushed his paddles deep into the oncoming waves. As he closed in on a tall pier, he noticed red painting on a cliff face. It was over 5,000 years old. He edged onto the white clamshell beach, where the BC Forestry Service had installed a sea wall in 1958.

The tide was moving away from shore, and *Ayak* beached low. Billy quickly dragged it to the dock's edge. The low cloud started to precipitate; Billy's arms were already wet from the paddling. He found shelter in a small house not far from the shoreline. The home-owners had invited him to stay the night after seeing him paddle in — they hadn't expected to see a kayaker in December; kayaking in winter just wasn't done. The fire, beer and hot food made for a perfect ending to the day.

Sitting on the end of the dock at high tide, Billy unfolded a letter he had written to Urs while on Eden Island. The ink had smudged, so he copied it onto a new piece of paper.

> Sorry I've taken so long to write. I guess I'm not a very good writer. Hope you can forgive me there, friend.
>
> I camped on a small group of islands called the Burdwoods and did up a large quantity of clams and my next winter's soup-mix. The soup-mix consists of the following, dried: nettles, balsam-fir sprouts, wild onions, seaside plantain, wild peas, wild carrot tops and sea lettuce. The clams I did as following: I dug up a large sack-full and let them soak in sea water for a few days so they could clean themselves. Then I steamed them open in my large s.s. pot. Then I put them through my meat grinder along with fresh wild onions and patted this mixture into patties (like hamburgers). These I smoke/dried.
>
> Now I am just gathering my daily meals and fishing, waiting for the berries to start happening so I can get my fruit supply together. Then I'll have next win-ter's food supply done. After that I may head north towards Alaska or something. Who knows where ever the wind and tides take me — ha! ha!

Oh! Upon getting back to the Simoom Sound area, I went to see some old friends of mine. I found they had a parcel for me. It was from you. As it turned out, the parcel arrived just after I had left for Calgary. Thanks so very much Urs for the guidebook, photo, coffee, sugar and that Swiss candy. Thanks so much there buddy!!

In an introspective passage, Billy admitted that he still felt the pull of his former life:

I sure miss climbing with you and sure miss the Rockies... I still have that picture of u taken in the good old Yamnuska parking lot just before we went on CMC Wall. Every time I look at it, I sure get longings to be back out there climbing with you. Sorry I was so out of shape the last time out.

I sometimes think about moving back to Calgary and finding a job and getting into climbing again. But that somehow seems like taking a step backwards — if you follow me. I am just beginning to really get into living off the land and am now doing it fairly efficiently (the only domesticated stuff I use now is a little flour, some coffee from time to time and tobacco). Also, I would find it hard giving up the kayak. We've been through a lot in four years and a lot of water has passed under it.

Billy mailed the letter from the post office in Little Simoom Sound (Marijuana Bay), where bald eagles perched to eat salmon. The post office opened in 1912 on the Wishart Peninsula facing Echo Bay. In 1943, the post office moved to Gilford Island and then, in 1967, it moved a final time, to Simoom Sound. During the early 1900s, there was a small logging town there, with a stone school and even a basketball court. That was all gone when Billy arrived.

He then reconnected with his Austrian friend George Jahn and his German wife, Suzy, and hand-delivered them some eulachon oil. Suzy's father was a German physicist who lived in Costa Rica; she once brought him some eulachon oil for him to study. Chemical analysis revealed that the oil is full of amphetamines, a stimulant that if used too much can lead to illness. It's also the key ingredient in the drug speed.

Billy rigged up a small camp nearby to stay a while. One warm evening, he paddled out to visit George and Suzy and play music. A number of other people were visiting. One of them was a woman named Lori, who had arrived by boat from a logging camp in the Broughton Archipelago. They sang and drank until the moon dipped below the horizon.

Later that week, Billy was told that the owner of the logging camp where Lori was staying was making unwanted advances towards her. It didn't sit well with Billy. So one day he paddled up to the dock at the logging camp to take Lori away. The owner took exception and physically threatened him. That wasn't a good idea. Billy laid the owner out with a stern punch to the face before he and Lori ran to the kayak and paddled away. As Lori puts it today, "He paddled up and saved me."

They stayed on George and Suzy's float house for a while. During the day, they went fishing for halibut, which Billy had learned to find with his nose: he could smell where they were swimming. Lori said that as soon as Billy smelled some, he'd drop a line and have a fish on it instantly. They'd cook the fish with salal berries and share it with George and Suzy, then dry large amounts to rehydrate later. During down time, Billy used Reeves watercolours to create landscape paintings on plain paper. He'd give them to his friends or add them to the growing collection he kept on a small shelf.

Billy and Lori hoped to buy a float house, and they mentioned this to friends — including Bernadette and Tim Turner, who worked in float camps. When Tim heard that a nearby camp was shutting down, he extracted an old float from it, floated it over, and sold it to Billy and Lori for $400. Lori had to borrow the money from her parents. The float had a wood stove, and Billy strung up blue tarps for shelter.

They settled into a simple, happy life in Pierre's Bay. The area was named after Pierre Landry, who met his wife, Tove, in Montreal in 1977 while working in the film industry; with only a few dollars to their name, the couple took a train to Vancouver. In Nanaimo, they saw a posting for "a caretaker of a hunting and fishing resort in Echo Bay on Gilford Island... accessible only by boat or plane." Pierre was 25 when they got the job. It was a crash course in wilderness survival — "from city slicker to the boondocks," as he put it. There was only one dock, and the post office and store were on a log float. A plane came three times a week for the mail, and the freight came by boat. Six months later, Pierre and Tove towed their shack to Drury Inlet to caretake a logging camp. After staying in a few more bays, the couple, now with an infant son, ended up a few kilometres north of Echo and tied up. They named it Pierre's Bay. You could do that in the 1970s. For two years, Pierre boated the nearby children to school. They'd pass whales and orcas nearly every day. Decades later, they built a marina in Pierre's Bay, and sometime after that, they became the sole owners of Pierre's Echo Bay Lodge and Marina.

Billy and Lori's group of friends in Pierre's Bay and Echo Bay grew over the seasons. In 1981, Lori got pregnant. It did little to interrupt their daily routine of fishing and chores. She was hoping to give birth on their float house, but after nearly two days of labour, she needed to get to a hospital. Their friend Jim O'Donnell had a float plane. This would be Billy's first ever trip in an airplane.

A fierce storm was blowing in from the northwest. As heavy rain fell on the plane, the propeller cut through dense fog. As the plane tipped and toppled from side to side, hundreds of feet above the water, Lori screamed in pain and squeezed Billy's hand. Jim landed the plane at the harbour in Campbell River.

A few hours later, Lori gave birth to their son. They named him Westerly, after the westerly winds that always brought the nicest weather, and that would bring Billy home.

Chapter 17

KAYAK BILL

People cannot comprehend, could never understand me,
I'm sure. Something impelled this wanderlust.
—*ALOHA WANDERWELL*

BILLY AND LORI RETURNED TO THEIR FLOAT
house with Westerly. Pierre's Bay had become a bust-
ling place, with more boat traffic arriving every year.
Resorts were opening on many shorelines, like Nimmo
Bay, north of Pierre's. The new decade also saw an
expansion of the salmon farm industry into territories north of Port McNeill. Modern steel pen systems
replaced old wooden pens. They were an absolute
eyesore, according to Billy.

Recreational kayaking was going through a small
boom. New outfitters and retailers were opening from
Seattle to Vancouver. In 1980, John Dowd opened a store
on Granville Island called Ecomarine. He sold a number
of brands and introduced folding kayaks from Europe.
John coined the term "sea kayaking" and published
Sea Kayaking: A Manual for Long-Distance Touring in
1981. Before then, it was known as kayak-touring. Brian
Henry opened Ocean River Sports in Victoria in 1981.

Around that time, a number of industry members had a meeting in Seattle and formed the Trade Association of Sea Kayaking (TASK). They studied commercial sea kayaking to understand how businesses could thrive. While windsurfing was much more popular in the early 1980s, sea kayaking was slowly gaining popularity along the Pacific Northwest.

One warm afternoon, Billy sat on the float house in a wooden chair next to a small table. On the table was a sheet of paper, on which he was painting the Viner River, which flowed into the ocean east of their float house. Before the paint was dry, Billy laid masking tape onto the portions of the picture depicting water. When he peeled the tape away, it created the illusion of waves.

Suddenly, he stopped painting and looked off into the distance. He told Lori that he was going fishing and paddled away. Moments later, a group of kayakers rounded the corner into Pierre's Bay. They wanted to meet Kayak Bill, but Billy was already well out of sight. He returned once the group of paddlers was gone.

Billy's reputation as a bold solo kayaker was prompting other paddlers to seek him out. The many new kayakers on the coast were interested in Billy's intimate knowledge of the unmapped waters north of Vancouver Island. It happened more than once, kayakers showing up to meet Kayak Bill. The attention bothered him.

Eventually, he and Lori sold their float house to Francine and John Brower and moved to Sointula, a small community on Malcolm Island. Located off the northeast shore of Vancouver Island, the 24-kilometre-long, three-kilometre-wide island had a population of around 500. Orcas made regular stops at its smooth-pebble beaches, drawing crowds to the shoreline.

Sointula was founded by Finnish immigrants working at Nanaimo coal mines in the early 1900s. The group invited political philosopher Matti Kurikka to help build a town with utopian ideals. They founded the Kalevan Kansa Colonization Company and *Aika* newspaper, and negotiated with the government for land. In 1901, they took possession of the 28,000-acre island. Sointula, "place of harmony," continued to grow until Matti left with half of the colony in 1904. The remaining families kept their plots, and the government took the island back. Many of the original Finnish immigrants' descendants still live in town.

Sointula was a safe place to raise a child. Westerly could go to school, and Lori could find a job in town. But Billy didn't take to life in Sointula, so he built a small cabin on someone's backlot in Mitchell Bay, farther east on the island. He sometimes visited town to see Lori and Westerly; he also played music in a band at a pub called the Bilge, in the basement of a two-storey hotel next to the ferry dock. His circle of friends included George Jahn, Jim the pilot, Robbie Boise and Stewart Marshall, a paddler and painter. Some of his friends formed a band called Livingroom and recorded albums.

Billy's fascination with techno-mechanical objects led him to build a synthesizer, similar to an instrument he had built in Calgary. He collected dials, wires and knobs from anywhere he could. It took him a few months, but he built the box, generator, oscillator, modules, sequencers and more. He spent hours playing music on it, some of which was featured on the Livingroom album *Weather Permitting*.

As the years went by, Billy spent less and less time on Malcolm Island. On one visit, he was house-sitting when he got a phone call from his old friends Brian and Nancy Greenwood. Nancy later recalled:

> In 1987, Brian and I sailed his 27-foot sailboat *Yamnuska* through all the islands off northern Vancouver Island. We stopped to see Rob Wood on Maurelle Island, and he gave us a contact phone number for Bill. Sailed to Malcolm Island and phoned, and he answered! It was a fluke, because he was house-sitting and was only there to feed a friend's cat.
>
> We went over, and it was an old schoolhouse that he was house-sitting. I was glad to be on land for a bit, so I stayed there while Brian and Bill sailed to Village Island to see the house poles and other carvings.
>
> The night before we left Malcolm Island, Bill worked on his music synthesizer. On the back, all the little connectors had "washers" he had cut out of a Cameo tobacco can, dozens of these intricate tiny circles with donut holes. That says a lot about Bill's personality.

After Nancy and Brian's visit, Billy's solo paddling trips increased in duration from a few weeks to a few months. Every day was different. To be self-sufficient, he had to plan each day's food and supplies. He made new friends along the way, but mostly stuck to himself. He paddled the islands and coves around Broughton Archipelago and visited Gilford Island on a number of occasions. He hiked around the island, past an old village once inhabited by the Kwakwa̱ka'wakw. Under the thick bush were traces from a logging camp founded in 1918. Stacks of timber hid the shoreline; they were decades old and rotting from all sides. Next to them was a steam donkey engine once used for loading logging trucks — a relic of more prosperous years. Gilford Island had a healthy population of coho salmon that spawned all winter, unlike coho found elsewhere, which spawned only once a year. It took Billy almost no time at all to catch salmon using a big, shiny spoon as a lure.

Late one winter's evening, Billy returned to his Gilford Island camp. He had little time to rig a tarp over the bed he had built the previous year. The fog was a little like rain, but more like snow. He shivered into his sleeping bag. There was no keeping the fire lit. The damp air felt colder than an Alberta winter. Billy's clothes were soggy and his hands clammy. He didn't sleep much. In the morning, the fog lifted to reveal snow-capped trees, their branches bent under the weight. Billy changed into dry clothes. By noon, he was warm and eating salmon. As the snow line climbed up the mountain sides, he lit a big fire to dry his heavy outfit.

During the darkest days of winter, the cold continental air that flowed out of the inlets would run into the moist Pacific weather moving up from the south, generating big clouds that unloaded huge amounts of snow. Billy soon found out that on the coldest of winter days, even the ocean would freeze.

Billy sometimes sheltered in Viner Sound, where wolves would stand on the shore and watch him paddle past, and swans wintered every year. Viner was the site of ancient villages. Dilapidated buildings once used for salmon chumming were all that remained.

He would sometimes head to the Burdwood Group, a collection of 17 islands west of Tribune Channel. In the spring, the islands had beautiful flowers, herons and kingfishers. The home of Guy Lawson, the first European to live on the island, was still there. On the western point, Billy found a Kwakwa̱ka̱'wakw village built nearly 8,000 years ago.

On one visit, he realized that there was little to no water supply and he couldn't dig a well, so he relied on the scant freshwater he had brought. After a few days under sunny skies, and two paintings, Billy needed water, so he went to Marijuana Bay. He paddled into the heart of the sound, past Louisa Islet and Esther Point, and drifted to shore at Simoom Sound Creek, where George Vancouver once noted: "The sea has now changed from its natural, to river coloured water, the probable consequence of some streams falling into the bay, or into the ocean to the north of it, through the low land."

Billy stayed in Echo Bay for a month before leaving for Kingcome Inlet. He was up before sunrise every day to make coffee and write in his journal. In one of his only notes that survived from that year, Billy wrote:

> Up at sunrise to mostly clear skies and light north-
> east wind. Tide at highwater slack. Decided to head
> out. Didn't take too long to break camp, get every-
> thing down to the beach and load *Ayak*. Tide had
> only fallen a couple of feet and it was looking good
> for the paddle to Gregory Island. I was feeling pretty
> good, too. By the time I reached the open water, a
> northwester had sprung up so I headed back. Didn't
> have far to pack everything back up the beach cause
> the tide had only fallen about four feet. Once moved
> in, no tarps, had a smoke and coffee break plus this

entry. Luckily didn't try to continue cause strong northwest gusts here at camp. High scattered cloud coming from the direction. Maybe tomorrow will be better so I'll not put any tarps up and only unpack things when I need them and then re-pack them again when I'm finished with their use.

After the above entry, I finished two left-over pancakes, had a good poo and then walked trail on a hunting/gathering trip. Hot once again with the sky clearing. Headed along the beach to next deep bay to the northeast and scared a couple of ravens. Back at the camp, I got a fire going for tea.

Two days after that, Billy departed for Gregory Island. He was paddling into waters where kayakers were so rare that he might have been one of the first. The mountains were bigger, and the trees were taller, than on Gilford Island. It was a rainforest, with waterfalls pouring into the ocean down granite walls. Over the next few years, he travelled farther up the coast and away from Broughton. Whenever he returned, he'd paddle past Donegal Head and into Mitchell Bay. His returns grew farther and farther apart as he pushed his camps north towards Bella Bella.

When he visited Malcolm, he'd bring Westerly to his cabin. Westerly remembers the smell of Billy's Drum tobacco and pot cigarettes. On one visit, when Westerly was nearly 10, Billy took him for a four-day walk around Malcolm Island. It was a sort of initiation into the wilderness. Every night before bed, Billy read to Westerly from *The Lord of the Rings*. When Westerly was 12, his dad took him for a paddle; Westerly used his mom's boat. Something went wrong and Westerly's kayak flipped and spat him out into the cold Pacific. Billy got Westerly and his kayak to shore and lit a big fire. He admonished Westerly to be aware of the dangers on the ocean.

Billy sometimes entertained Westerly with stories about his Yosemite visits. He told him about being high on El Capitan, stranded in a thunderstorm for days. He'd go into detail about how a helicopter wanted to rescue him but he called it off. He never told Westerly about the Rockies, Yamnuska or the CMC. He hardly talked about his life before the coast at all. He never really told Lori much about his past either. Well, except for the storm and helicopter on El Capitan. One day, during a conversation with Lori on the float house, Billy raised his voice and said, "You don't know everything about me." It was a moment that Lori wouldn't forget.

Billy didn't stay in touch with his brother, Ken, even though Ken was living on the west coast. Every once in a while, Billy's dad sent him a box of candy, but they never had any further correspondence. One year, Billy's friend Joel made him and Westerly matching hunting knives, Westerly's much smaller. Billy made a sealskin sheath for his and carried it everywhere. "That was the persona of Bill, his big knife," said Lori.

Billy never told anyone where he was going when he left Malcolm Island. He'd sometimes send letters to people like Rob, his old girlfriend Dianne and Urs in Calgary. Sometimes he'd run into old friends and give them a painting. He was averaging a few a month, and living room walls on Malcolm Island started to fill up with Kayak Bill paintings. By the early 1990s, Billy had established camps at Cape Caution, Extended Point,

Grief Bay and all the way up to Bella Bella. After Cape Caution are the outer islands, a place too far for eco-tourists. There's no logging out there.

Billy's camps had become more sophisticated, and he'd developed a system that other paddlers would soon be able to recognize as indicating a Kayak Bill camp. He sometimes visited town to get supplies like tobacco, garlic, rolling papers, rice, flour and ammunition for his .22. His kayak was packed with everything he needed.

In the fall of 1994, Billy made regular visits to a small, remote logging barge in the Finlayson Channel between Klemtu and Bella Bella, near Milbanke Sound. The men working on it visit town to get supplies only once every four to six weeks. The 10-by-30-metre barge had a number of trailers on it; cables connected it to shore to keep it in a sheltered place. It had no phone, only a VHF radio. There was little boat traffic in the channel except for a few fishing rigs.

One of the men on the barge was Colin Lake, who was in his early 20s. After camp chores, Colin went fishing or hiking. His boss had told him that Billy might come around. One morning, Billy paddled in, looking weathered and fit. He was wearing all wool and had a long beard and curly hair. Colin made them eggs and coffee. In the kitchen, Billy smoked his hand-rolled cigarettes and looked over his well-used charts and tide schedule, which he checked every day. In such a hostile environment, every decision had to be planned out. Billy told Colin he chose which of his camps to use based on the season and number of tourists.

From time to time, Colin ran into other kayakers looking for Billy, but he told them he'd never heard of Kayak Bill. During Christmas break one year, when the barge was left empty, Billy took care of it. After a few weeks away, Colin and his co-workers found everything in perfect order, and their camp dog had been switched to a seal diet.

By the mid-1990s, Billy had camps that extended far up the coast, past Bella Bella. Some were full-time shelters where he lived for months; others were bivy camps for brief stopovers. He almost never visited Malcolm Island anymore. The last time Westerly saw his father was in 1996. Lori took some photos of Billy sitting on their front porch; they turned out a little blurry. Billy continued to move his camps farther north, away from the new fish farms and increasing boat traffic. He never stopped painting.

Chapter 18

THE PAINTER

The painter doesn't try to reproduce the scene before him...
he simplifies and eliminates until he knows exactly what
stirred him, sets this down in color and line as simply and
as powerfully as possible and so translates his impression
into an aesthetic emotion.

—*DAVID MILNE*

BILLY MADE A HANDWRITTEN DRAFT FOR EVERY climbing journal he made. He then typed the journals using a typewriter. He would sometimes cut the handwritten drafts into squares to be used as backing for pictures that he taped into his journals. That was in 1960. A few years later, he started sketching small animals and birds. When he took over as the editor of the CMC newsletter, he was drawing on a regular basis. In the early 1970s, he was sketching self-portraits using ink and pencil. His first painting, oil on canvas, was made after he and Ian Heys made the fourth ascent of Balrog, on Yamnuska. It depicts himself and other CMC members standing next to Shadowfax, Gandalf's horse, in front of a balrog — the *Lord of the Rings* beast for which the route was named. It hangs in Perry Davis's home.

Billy also took a lot of photos and video footage in the early 1970s. He even started his own production company, WLD Productions, making short slideshows that were shown at CMC meetings. In the mid-1970s, he painted on whatever paper he could find. He transitioned from recording his life on camera to expressing his vision of the world around him through art. He drew his inspiration from nature. "His paintings were more than just a stylistic representation of nature," said Perry. "They have a spiritual quality." One of his first paintings, which he sent to Urs in Calgary, depicted Knight Inlet with a giant foot in front of it, the toes gripping a rope. At the bottom, it read, "Artafishyouall climbing."

Billy met Stewart Marshall in the mid-1970s near Sointula. They shared a love for paddling, but more importantly, they shared a love for painting. Stewart was born three years before Billy; when he was 10 years old, living in Montreal with his three siblings, he stretched out an old bedsheet and painted on it with oils. After high school, he hitchhiked to Mexico, then went on an extended canoe trip in Quebec. It was there that Stewart met Edmond Gaudette, a trapper and paddler who was impressed with Stewart's paddling skills and invited him to be his assistant. "When I went in," said Stewart, "I was just a green city boy. When I left, I could survive in the woods with just a knife. I always had my watercolours and brushes with me." Art school at Sir George Williams University, now Concordia University, improved his technical skills.

He took a train to Vancouver from Montreal in 1972 and soon found himself living in a hut on the coast. He built a 6.5-metre kayak that he named *Burdwood* and

rigged up with a sail that allowed it travel very fast —
on one trip, he was nearly flung into the water because
Burdwood's speed caused its bow to dip with such force.
With his old friend from Vancouver, George Dyson — the
same one who had patented the Frontiersman kayak
— Stewart paddled 1600 kilometres north to Glacier
Bay, Alaska.

In 1977, when Stewart was building a float house
outside of Sointula, he and Billy met at a mutual
friend's float. The cold weather was getting to Stewart,
and the following summer he bought a sailboat
named *Jesymara* and sailed to Maui. He returned to
Canada a few years later but made regular trips to
the tropics. On one of them, he brought Billy's synthesizer to play during quiet time on the water. A master
violinist, Stewart would sometimes accompany the
synthesizer on fiddle. As gulls squawked, the electric
vibrations from Billy's instrument rippled across the
ocean. Stewart left the synthesizer with someone in
Hawaii, and locals say that it still sends sounds into
the night air.

Stewart captured the landscapes around him with
pencils and watercolours in a representational style;
some of his paintings appeared in small galleries in
Vancouver. When he paddled, he brought a logbook that
he'd use to sketch trees and shorelines, later recreating
the scenes on full or quartered 56-by-76-centimetre
sheets of watercolour paper. On longer trips, he'd bring
40 small tubes of watercolour paint and 20 large ones
of acrylic — Windsor & Newton watercolours, he said,
were the best. Representation became less important to
Stewart as time went on; instead he wanted to capture
the power of what he was seeing.

He doesn't paint anymore. His wormhole-ridden two-storey shed on the beach in Sointula continues to rot. He had to tear down his art studio because it crept onto municipal land. He rebuilt a stand-up bass which he continued to play into his mid-70s. At the party nights in the Bilge, Stewart would play mandolin in the band with Billy.

Billy wanted to kayak the Pacific Rim, and he would ask Stewart about his trip to Alaska and how the paddling was that far north. Stewart told him stories and shared insights from his abundant experience on the water. He'd had many close calls with death.

Once, crossing Queen Charlotte Sound in November in another kayak he'd built, named *Ahti*, he found himself in the Goose Islands, hoping to catch a westerly wind that could bring him south to Malcolm. A big groundswell came from the open Pacific to the northwest. He was in a 15-foot swell when a strong outflow wind from the Queen Charlotte Strait slammed into him. The winds were blowing *Ahti* to the west in a five-foot wind chop. He paddled through the night under a full moon and approached Nahwitti Bar, where the sea can build into walls of water. The orange moon shining through the waves looked like blood. He was being blown into waters he had no charts for. He lost control of *Ahti* when a wave broke over him nearly 20 kilometres off shore. Borderline hypothermic in the freezing weather, Stewart accepted that he might die. Just then a crashing wave doused him with a frigid blast of ocean.

He thought of his friends and family. He had to make it to Fisherman Bay or risk being pushed out to sea. He paddled with everything he had, and 24 hours after setting off, reached the bay. Big groundswells were smashing waves against the rocky shore. His rudder had broken sometime during the night. He managed to ram *Ahti* into a high-tide mark and jumped out. He took off his heavy soaked pants off and grabbed the bowline. He spent a week under frosted trees, repairing his boat, before heading off again.

Standing in his falling-apart shack, which had once stood as a proud workshop and studio, Stewart spoke about his encounters with Billy:

> He was living in Mitchell Bay and selling a lot of paintings, and our mutual friend Rob Marino dubbed him "dollar bill" after he started to sell them. We all laughed about that.
>
> He heard me talk about the areas north of Bella Bella. He made a painting of me there, not having been there but imagining it. Soon, he was heading up. We were always in the same territory up north, Billy and I. Sometimes we would paddle past one another. You see, I could cover in a day what he could cover in three weeks because of my sail. So sometimes I'd see him a few times in a short period of time. Once, he was paddling down Seaforth Channel and I was paddling up. He was leaving one of his camps. I found his camp and left him these gigantic footprints in the sand. Big sasquatch feet with dug-out toes. There was a wolf there next to me while I did it.
>
> I would always leave things there for Billy in his camps. I take enough with me to live the rest of my life. If I get bound to shore, I have wire, cord, sacks of rice. Whenever I knew I was going home, I'd leave

a note at his camp with rice, oats and sugar. That extends your time so much, it means you don't have to go somewhere and get anything. Now you can stay for months.

I always knew where he was. In the early spring, we'd start our season up Knight Inlet. All of the eagles and seals headed up for the big feed. The eulachon season is the first full moon of April. Fishing was a just a way to eat, but I could troll really well. I could live aboard my kayak and cook on it. I could even get out and go for a swim. Billy couldn't do any of that because he had a smaller boat. I'm a bit of a packrat, so the weight kept the boat in place. I was the only one ever doing that. I don't think anyone has ever kayaked from here to Queen Charlotte and back, alone. The longest push I ever did was 185 kilometres. I would have to carry so many charts. During my last year of paddling, I got a GPS, which meant no more charts. But it got rid of a lot of weight.

Stewart and Billy sometimes shared fires on remote shorelines. They would enjoy coffee and smokes. They had both perfected making what Stewart called "camp coffee"—like cowboy coffee, it simply consists of grounds in boiling water. To make it perfectly, Stewart said, you need to bring the water almost, but not totally, to a boil, then let it cool down until it's fizzy. Sprinkle the coffee over the water slowly but don't stir it. Put the lid on and wait for five minutes until there's foam, "the good stuff." No eggshells needed. Take the pot with the lid still on and shake it gently back and forth; the steamed grounds on top will throw out the remaining chocolatey foam. Then leave it for five minutes. The waterlogged grounds will sink to the bottom after five minutes. About ten minutes after the near-boil, it's finished. "The flavour is so rich."

Stewart and Billy never painted together, but Billy would sometimes show his work to Stewart. One of his paintings hung on the wall of Stewart's old shack. It depicted Billy himself paddling past the Ivory Island lighthouse in a crashing wave under the moonlight. Stewart would often just stare at it.

> His imagination was superior to mine. The way he looked at things and the way he put them together. He didn't stick with the redundancy of repeating a vision. He changed everything in his own way. Because of my technical skill, I always displayed what I saw and repeated it. He augmented things in a way that made them so special. He didn't have the drawing skills, like technically developed skills. Drawing is something that takes a lot of training, if you haven't been led to understand what it's all about — like transferring three dimensions into two — and understanding the line. I loved the way he would have swatches. He would test each colour carefully before putting them down. He would have pieces of paper he'd test them on.

> He didn't paint much out there [on kayak trips]. He painted when he was back at his winter camp. I'd paint what was out there in front of me. He learned to [get] the info and paint after. I keep his old paint box in my shop now. It's a little Tupperware container. He'd put good-quality dishrags in the bottom.

What I'm holding in my hand was Billy's rag. He'd put his paint tubes on top of the rag and his brushes. If you keep a little water in the rag, the container would have enough moisture so the tubes didn't dry out. I'd share my paints with him. Once every two years or so, I'd go to Vancouver and visit Opus Arts Supplies. I didn't see all of his paintings, but the ones I saw were remarkable.

Most of Billy's original paintings are in Mitchell Bay and Shearwater, but some went to auction and were listed for as much as $5,000. Some were made into prints. Lori always said that she wanted Billy's paintings to end up in a coffee table book, but tracking them all down would be nearly impossible.

Billy didn't paint like other watercolour painters; his works looked more like acrylic. With their bold colours and abstract subjects, they were sometimes described as a blend of Emily Carr's style with Pablo Picasso's. Billy portrayed clouds, ocean, trees and mountains layered with strong blues, purples, reds, oranges and yellows. The trees and rocks often contain images of faces and creatures. Different angles will reveal different elements.

In one painting, for example, a duck stands on a log, holding a stop sign. The small bird resembles doodles Billy did in the Archie Simpson hut logbook decades earlier. It appears to be floating on water, but when the image is flipped, the duck is in fact floating in an inverted image of white mountains and a black, starry night. Then there's the painting of two ravens on a log with a large grey island in the foreground and big mountains behind that, containing an image of a face.

The two ravens first appeared in Billy's journals when he was climbing in Calgary. A painting of Donegal Head on Malcolm Island takes a bird's-eye perspective. Billy had only ever flown in a plane once, when Westerly was born, but the detail is nearly perfect, with big trees, bright water and old timber washed onto shores.

Billy sometimes met with other painters to share ideas. Yvonne Maximchuk moved from White Rock to Echo Bay in the early 1980s with her partner and two children. She and Billy had a number of painting sessions together, sharing ideas. She went on to become a well-known artist and continued to live in Echo Bay, where she authored a number of books about living off the grid as a painter.

During their 1987 sailing trip to the west coast, Brian and Nancy Greenwood took the initiative of commissioning and purchasing art from Billy, and these efforts helped bring his paintings onto the walls of Urs and other Alberta friends. Nancy recalled:

> I visited a little gallery in Sointula and met a woman named Jackie, who handled Bill's paintings and brought in art supplies for him. Back in Duncan, we contacted Jackie because we wanted to buy one of Bill's paintings. Bill was no longer in the little schoolhouse, so we had to go through Jackie. She mailed the painting. That's the one that Perry has. Then Brian talked to Jackie and told her he wanted Bill to paint him mountains and ocean. Some weeks later we received the magical one that Urs now has. We loved it. Look for the totemic figures Bill has hidden in the rocks and mountains.

When Brian knew he was going to die, one thing he was grateful for was that he had the time to give his favourite things to his friends. He had already given Jack Firth a painting of Cloggy given to him years earlier by Ginger Cain, an old friend from Llanberis. And so, when Jack and Georgina were visiting us, Brian and Jack wrapped Bill's paintings for Jack to deliver to Perry and to Urs. A very emotional experience for us all.

The paintings Billy made for Brian and Nancy are similar to many of his others, but one of them has much more detail in the mountains. It depicts an evening setting; soft light reveals snowy slopes on coastal mountains and green forests below. The ocean is calm, at low tide. Another portrays a choppy brownish ocean and rolling hills with a few hidden faces, and a series of blue clouds on an orange sky.

His final paintings were made in Shearwater. They portrayed angular rock features, rows of trees and breaking waves. His last one was on a full sheet of watercolour paper — the first time he'd used a full sheet. The unsettled bluish water ripples away from small rocks protruding up from the shore. A marshy area gives way in the mid-ground to bushy terrain with trees, their branches facing inland. In the back-right corner is a dark sky with a moon, but to the left is a bright sky with faded peaks. It hangs on a wall in Shearwater.

No one knows for sure how many paintings Billy did, but Lori believes there are thousands. They paid for his day-to-day essentials. He left something of himself in each one, a memory or an experience. After passing them along on his seasonal trips to town, he would paddle away to the wilderness, sometimes for five months. On the darkest and coldest nights, with ground-swell crashing on rocks near his camp, Billy likely took some solace in knowing that somewhere, someone was looking at one of his paintings, peering into his world and imagining what wild landscape he was immersed in. Sometimes, even if you're alone, you can be happy knowing someone out there is thinking about you.

Chapter 19

OUTSIDE PASSAGE

You come into the world alone and you go out of the world alone yet it seems to me you are more alone while living than even going and coming.

—*EMILY CARR*

BILLY'S JOURNALS FROM THE 1980S AND 1990S were kept in a trailer behind a friend's home. At some point, a friend of that friend found the journals badly water damaged and, not knowing their significance, threw them away. In those journals were hundreds of Billy's daily entries, drawings of edible plants and charts to his camps. While some of Billy's travels during those years are well documented, the intimate information of his life is lost forever. In one dramatic passage that does survive, he describes a storm he experienced while caretaking at a beachcomber's float camp in Lambard Inlet, north of Bella Bella:

> Had some real wild weather looking after that camp and one winter experienced a hurricane. I was woken up by the shaking of the trailer. Got up, switched the light on (had 12 volt lighting when the

gen-set wasn't running), made a big brew of instant java, rolled a Drum then headed out. A savage gust blew a sheet of steel weighing between hundred and fifty to two hundred pounds off the burn barrel and into the seas. No sooner had my foggy mind registered that when another crash caused my head to swivel into the wind. Just caught a glimpse of the tug's oil stove chimney landing in almost the gen-set's fuel supply (around thirty plastic five-gallon containers of gasoline). Luckily, the stove had blown out a couple days before and I hadn't been able to get it going again. So, didn't have to crawl down into the bow to shut it off. The tug was tipping back and forth violently cause of the two-foot breaking waves which had built up from ripplets along the lee of the line of boom-sticks used as a breakwater, in about two hundred feet. Just then, a break in the racing clouds revealed a just-past-full moon and night became day. It spot-lighted the blowing spray just the other side of Leighton Island and what a wild looking sight. The spray contrasted well with the inky black clouds coming in over Lady Douglas Island. Noticed a line of various objects bobbing their way to the back of the bay and adding to the line of bric-a-brac along the high-water line.

There was an updated version of the lighthouse's reports on the marine forecast (normally they stop reporting in at 10:30 p.m.) and when they got to Ivory Island's station, it was reporting wind gusts of up to 99 knots with 10 metre (30 foot) N.W. wind waves crossing 10 metre S.W. running swell; a combination during the big sets would reach 60 feet. Glancing down on the living room rug, noticed Blackie, a fat little furry cat and Teddy, a sort of giant sausage with short legs and a miniature shepherd's head, glaring up at me as if to say, "cut the lights."

Did eventually get back to sleep when the wind began to drop-off at the falling of the tide.

In the late 1990s, Billy moved to Shearwater, on Denny Island, and almost never ventured south. He sometimes visited Mitchell Bay to bring paintings to friends. In 1999, he visited Lori and her new husband, Bob, but didn't get a chance to see Westerly. Billy and Bob spent an afternoon together, sharing stories.

Billy made new friends on Denny Island. He had built a complex series of camps along the outer islands, where he spent most of his time. On one of those islands, he told a friend in Shearwater, he awoke one morning to a wolf sitting next to him. Billy shared seal meat with the wolf, which kept him company for a few weeks. Then, as suddenly as it had arrived, the wolf was gone.

He'd established dozens of camps over the years. Some of his favourites were on islands such as Eden, Denny, Goose, Ivory, Cecilia, Aristazabal (where he had three), Dufferin, Dallas, the Roar Islets and Hunter Island (where he had two, one at Mustang Bay and one at Swordfish Bay). Some were complex, with intricate systems, and others were simple. Back in Shearwater one summer, Billy opened charts that showed details on coastlines from Malcolm Island up to the Bella Bella area. He used a pen to mark where his camps were. He also made small notes on tides and when to travel to them.

Because Billy had a heavily laden double kayak, moving forward in wind and chop was difficult. His crossings had to be as short as possible, which meant he had to be able to predict the conditions for up to three hours. When he left Shearwater, he would head north and then nearly as far west as he could go in a day. He took a number of paddling routes. Sometimes he would paddle to Dufferin Island and head from there to Dallas Island, where he would stay for a few days. Then he would paddle south through Milbanke Sound and back north on the western shore of Price Island to his Higgins Passage camp. From there he would paddle to one of his three camps on Aristazabal Island. The name Aristazabal came from a group of Spanish sailors who, in 1792, became the first Europeans to visit the island. George Vancouver later used the name on his English charts. From there, Billy paddled across open ocean to his Harvey Islands camp. He would live there for up to three months. Billy kept his marked-up charts with his journals in Shearwater. They revealed just a small glimpse into his routines and voyages.

Glenn Lewis is the only other paddler to have explored the area as much as Billy. "Bill and I came from a time that predates the sports paddling trend that got going about 20 years ago that now dominates the padding community," said Glenn, who continued to paddle into his 70s.

> The old approach was more about avoidance of risk than gaining more technical skills and equipment to handle rougher conditions. It's so isolated up there where Billy camped, you're on your own. You have to look out for yourself or it won't work out. People that

I know who spent as much time alone as Billy, well, some of them suffered from attachment disorder.

As Billy wrote in his journal, spending that time alone became more and more difficult as the area became busier:

Ran into a couple of kayakers who were heading to Bella Bella. They told me that they had just come from some new cabins at the south entrance to Gale Passage. I got the impression that they had been built by the Heiltsuk people for the fast-increasing tourist kayak trade. That whole triangle of the Goose, Hunter and Bardswell island group was getting extremely busy in the summer. Goose Island and part of Hunter Island being now a national park.

Thank god I had the luck to be there 15 to 20 years ago when one could still live off the land and feel what it was like before the coming of man and his machine. I remember spending whole winters there and not seeing a soul and only the odd plane and boat off in various directions. And the living was real good. Lots of fat little deer and geese, goose tongue (seaside plantain), wind peas, a little sea asparagus and the wild fruit: huckleberries, high bush blueberries, wild crab apples plus the usual salal. It was paradise. But that's another story.

Billy arrived back in Shearwater in February 2001 after spending five months away at his camps. He built a tiny cabin on the backlot of Andrea and Bryan Clerx's home and settled in there. He wrote in his journal about clearing the land to build it, and about collecting money from people who owed him from the previous fall. From March until June, he spent about 30 days painting. He finished his cabin and wrote about where the moon was and the weather. He went to Bella Bella for supplies, visited friends and took regular naps. His journal entries were short, point-form notes in tiny calendar boxes. On May 12 he spent $20 on pizza, and on May 30 he read from *The Lord of the Rings*. He finished a number of paintings and earned nearly $2,000 by the end of June.

On July 24, Billy made a note about writing a letter to Westerly, but Westerly said he never received any such letter. For six days in July, he prepared for his next trip. During the first few weeks of August, he practised loading *Ayak* before paddling off again towards the northwest. Recapping his trip in journal entries written a year later, he described setting off:

> First light found me loading-up old *Ayak* at the foot of a concrete ramp in Shearwater, BC. Overcast (high fog), a little drizzle and a light southerly helped to keep me cool as I packed 400 pounds of grub-stake down to the waterline, which of course was at its low tide extreme — ha! ha! ha!
>
> Was pretty oblivious to my surroundings, as I had a mental image of the two practice loadings on Andrea and Bryan's front lawn recycling through my brain. Was no mean feat jamming that much stuff into a kayak (general order of packing is shown in diagram below) and time it was done, old *Ayak* had about ½ inch of freeboard and the tide was just starting to rise.

Was heading for my Dufferin Island Camp, which meant bucking a new moon flood, and thought of it wasn't very pleasant. Turned out to be not too bad, as I was able to make use of some fine back-eddies. The worst spot turned out to be right at the start of the trip, on the N.E. side of a small island between Shearwater and the fish plant.

Stopped for a smoke and coffee break in the chain of small islands which protect the large body of water fronting Bella Bella, then headed across the boat lane to Dryad Point light house. After a short paddle, one can duck-in behind several medium sized islands and the narrow channels between them and the N.W. side of Campbell Island, had some really strong back eddies; so was making really good time. Would paddle hard for about a dozen strokes, then just glide along with the current, enjoy another Drum and coffee break and watching the mossy shore go by. Lots of ducks around and the sea was smooth. Was only the odd sprinkle happening so didn't have to skirt-up or wear a rain jacket and it was still pretty cool. It sure felt good to be on the way out to the outside and for me that meant the west coast of Aristazabal Island and beyond.

Billy headed across Raymond Pass through intensifying rain, and made his way to Idol Point.

The bay below the camp had at its westerly arm, a point of old growth forest (mostly hemlock and spruce inland and hedged with huge cedars overhanging the beach) which ended abruptly in a large logged-off area covered in a riotous growth of salal, huckle, salmon and thimble berries. Small patches of alder bordered the skid-roads and parts of the beach front with here and there wild crab apples and miniature willows.

The easterly arm started as a steep rocky spit, sparsely covered in tall beach grass, which ran a short way to a tiny islet with one cedar growing out off a bed of bear berry. A few chocolate lilies and wild strawberries added colour to the scene and on some of the tiny ledges and shelves, little patches of goose tongue, stone-crop and moss.

The islet fanned-out towards the north in a reef of incredibly old rock which was broken-up in lots of narrow channels; these ending in steep pebble or sand beaches. The view that way was of Spiller Channel and the high snow-covered mainland mountains. Most of the time the stream at the upper beach was o.k. except when storms washed up pop weed (bladderwrack) and laid it in a fermenting carpet two feet deep over the fresh water.

Spent three days at this camp and was bothered by a few bugs (moskitoes and no-see-ums). Got out fishing once and only managed to catch two small cods before an out-flow out of Spiller Passage made it too windy to jig. Winds were all over the place and except for the southerlies, kept it reasonably cool. Had everything from drizzle to scattered showers with sunny breaks, so the weather wasn't too bad.

Did a nice long beach-walk towards Idol Point and saw some interesting geological features. The exposed rock is extremely old; having being missed by the last ice age, and the sea has cut great bays and gullies into the shelving rock. Moderate to steep beaches of fine sand, peagravel and small rock made hiking enjoyable. Took the odd side-trip out to the ends of the reefs and found some small patches of pretty big mussels. Overhanging the beach in many places was a wall of thimble berry bushes and they were laden with fruit. Spent some time among them. On the sunny sides of the points and near the storm tide line, were a few gooseberry bushes. Had a good feed of them. Wasn't much in the way of beach wood in that direction but didn't matter as the beach towards Gale Passage had lots. The last part of the stay was pretty noisy due to an almost endless succession of plane flights from Bella Bella to the sport fishing lodge in St. John Harbour. Added to that the seine fleet was scattered about from Idol Point to Ivory Island and with the still pretty busy cruise ship and yacht traffic, was glad to head for Dallas Island.

From Dallas Island, Billy next headed for Balagny Passage.

Ended up going in between the seine boat and the reef and as I cleared it someone shouted, "Hey, Kayak Bill." Didn't want to stop and quack as the tide was getting strong and the wind was picking up, so just gave them a salute with the paddle then poured on the coat. Had the skirt on but thankfully not the heavy Helly Hansen, as it was still looking like a dry S.E.er. Got a little sloppy in a few places

where the strong flood tide was opposing the building S.E. wind waves and the seas got pretty big just
off Balagny Passage.

Was glad to reach the sheltered waters of the pass,
where I could drift in on the flood and have a smoke
and coffee break. Real pretty though, that area, with
lots of grass flats and tiny islets, but not much beach
wood and bug heaven; so, one wouldn't camp there
except in an emergency. Being right beside the Don
Peninsula (mainland) and with the narrow passes,
it's not uncommon to see bears.

Eventually, Billy arrived at the same place where
he'd endured the hurricane in the beachcomber's cabin.

The longest I'd ever spent at this camp was while
waiting to get paid for a caretaking stint; same
beachcomber's camp I experienced that wild
weather in. It ended up being about three months
and by then was just about out of supplies. To
help pass the time, built two beautiful trails that
cross the island. Lots of boardwalks to sand during
arctic outflows and well-marked with fisherman
floats found beachcombing over the years. It was
almost a daily ritual to walk it at first light for
water. One breaks out on a large crescent beach
near its north end and is composed of fairly large
smooth rocks that steeply slant-up to the storm
tide line. With the global warming slowly raising
the sea level, the big swell is now pushing this rock
into the forest. Lots of beach wood at the regular
highwater line. As one heads to the S.W. end the

rocks get smaller till it's just fine pea-gravel below the spring. Seen lots of deer and wolf tracks there over the years.

Billy continued to write about his trip in the small boxes of his calendar. Over the next few weeks, he would keep track of the wind, bugginess, weather, moon and tides. On August 30, back at the Dallas Island camp, he gave himself a haircut and he found a number of glass balls. He also caught a dozen cod and spotted some deer. In September, he caught hundreds of mussels and moved to Higgins Pass camp, where a wolf kept him company, and then was on to Aristazabal III, which he had visited the year before. He experienced the strongest storm of the year and spent just over five days smoking a pack of Drum, waiting it out. He watched big whales swim by.

In October, he killed a seal and made one gallon of oil and 30 seal burgers. A few days later, he caught 70 mussels. On the 20th he went beachcombing, and on the 24th he got his first view of the blue moon. He then moved over to his Harvey Island camp. November 16 marked the day Billy had been out on this trip for three months, alone. He finished his seal blubber crispies, didn't see the sun for eight days and stayed busy working on his camp. On November 24, he paddled back to his Aristazabal III, where he caught more cod and mussels. In December, he was down to his last jars of sugar, pinto beans and seal oil. On December 14, he had a bad toothache and swelling in his mouth. He popped the inflammation and took rum, his first sip of alcohol since leaving four months earlier.

A few summers back, Stewart Marshall had taken Billy to a dentist in Sointula. Stewart gave the dentist some paintings in exchange for the work. The dentist took one look at Billy's teeth and said he wouldn't remove all of them — just most. Billy never returned.

On Christmas Day, he paddled to his Dallas Island camp. It was an "incredible day, a little rough at times in Milbanke Sound." By the end of the month, he was back in his cabin in Shearwater and started painting.

He paddled off again four months later.

> April 1, 2002 (Denny Island to Dufferin Island Camp):
>
> Rough (steep, breaking side-waves). Fish smell on the air. Lots of punt and gillnet boat traffic. Hundreds of seagulls on reefs near camp. Landed bone tired and sore just before high-water slack. Ducks and geese on beach. Camp in great shape with stream running good, odd herring carcass at high-water line. Leaves just forming on gooseberries.

Transferring to Dallas Island on April 7, he picked a path between fishing nets and spotted a coast guard vessel and some sea lions. The rain picked up before he made it to camp.

> Camp was in good shape and it didn't take long to get moved in. Hung pullover up to dry out but left rest of clothes to dry on me as I went for water. Stream running good and there was some recent beachcombing signs. Then got a roaring fire going to dry things out while doing this entry. Sure feels good to be here.

Eight days later, after "another really good poo," he struck out for his camp at Higgins Passage. It was wet and windy, with wind at times nearing gale force.

Thousands of seagulls around the entrance to Higgins Passage plus a small boat. Got a lot wetter with side-gusts as I paddled through the pass. Made the shortcut with the tide just starting to ebb. Lots of eagles and seals near the beach below the camp. Managed to get everything moved into camp without getting too wet and the camp was in good shape with the firewood dry. Was very tired and cold once I'd stopped rushing around, but a frying pan full of beans, rice and nuts with chapatis and grease plus a big brew of hot tea heavy with golden sugar warmed me up. Managed to go for the water plus make a new chapati dough before hitting the sack bone-tired.

On April 18, he continued to Aristazabal.

Just got through by the skin of *Ayak*'s bottom. Time I reached the beach below camp, the sun was disappearing on and off and the southerly was getting up to strong. Scared some geese off the low-water line as I landed. Camp in great shape but water hole half full of mud, leaves and sticks. Cleaned the well out. Then brewed two therms of tea and beefed-up the left-over cod stew with a little rice, cayenne pepper, garlic powder and grease (start of jar #4 of grease). It's another beautiful day! Thank you lord, sea and earth. A little firewood gathering, chopping, sawing plus bucket of fresh water before going to bed early with a sore lower back and hips.

Subsequent entries did not give updates on the back pain, but on June 13, 2002, Billy's dental troubles made another appearance ("loose tooth broke off during night"). But the big story that day was a happier one.

Tide was high enough to go out fishing with the northwesterly still blowing lightly but starting to pick up. Had a good poo just before heading out plus grabbed the rifle on an impulse. If it was too windy to fish would try seal hunting near the southeast entrance. Got four nice cod right away with the northwester up to medium. With the clams, figured that was enough and since there was still lots of highwater left, decided to try for a seal.

Paddled to the spot in the shortcut where I had seen some. Sure enough there was half a dozen playing in the shallows near a big rock. So I stopped paddling and let the wind and tide push me back behind that rock and out of their sight. There was a little swell on the rock but managed to land and tie *Ayak* off. While I got the rifle ready, noticed the seals out in the kelp patch watching me and every now and then one would do its warning slap. Was hoping that the seals on the other side of the rock weren't picking up on that. Climbed around the rock till I could see the spot. There were only two now, about forty feet away. Froze till they went under and then continued around and slightly down to a good spot to shoot from.

It was perfect. A sharp horizontal part of the rock with even a notch to rest the barrel in, plus a good place to stand. The wind was blowing my scent the other way and the lighting was good. And up they came. Took careful aim on the nearest one (about thirty feet away) and BANG, got him. Right away the other one dove (doing its warning slap) and three more popped up nearby looking around for the danger. The one I got was floating on the surface with blood starting to discolour the water. It wasn't moving at all so I knew it was a clean kill.

That was the first time that one didn't sink on me. Stood there for a moment not quite believing the scene, so used to missing I had become. Then I rushed back to the kayak cause it looked like I had a good chance of getting it right away and could tow it back instead of coming back later at lower water and either dragging it all the way back to the camp or dealing with it there; packing the meat and blubber back. Came around the same side of the rock as before and arrived just in time to see it drifting out on the other side, leaving a trail of blood behind it.

Caught up to it and tied each end of a short rope to each back flipper and the two line to that. Then tried heading out the short cut but it was too slow going bucking the current. So, stopped by an easy spot to get out of *Ayak*, laid the tarp I had been sitting on out along the bottom of the kayak, pulled the seal in and hauled it up out of the water and into the kayak. Was quite a grunt pushing it back into the back compartment. Was just able to get in again myself, as it didn't quite all fit in the back.

Had the hind flippers jammed in along side of me. That did the trick, however, and I made good time back to the camp.

After *Ayak* was cleaned out and put away (the tarp kept most of the blood off the bottom), the seal lugged up to the upper beach and laid on a tarp (which when folded over, covered it up), plus the cod hung, had a mug of tea plus a smoke while I calmed down. Then I cleaned and oiled the rifle and since I wouldn't be using it here again, oiled the inside of the barrel. Then this entry.

It wasn't until July 15 that Billy recorded any human interaction.

After eating, spent quite a while getting the journal caught up. Was partway through it when I heard someone yell, "Hello!" So went around to the north beach and found some Natives from Klemtu nosed up to the beach in a small boat. They had seen the smoke from my fire and wondered if I needed help. Told them I'd just come from Harvey Island where I'd spent 2.5 months and that my supplies were getting low. One of them bent down and came up with the whole hind leg of a deer which he threw onto the beach. After a short chat and many thanks, they motored off. It was then that I realized that was my first spoken words in 3.5 months.

That night, Billy ate deer meat "fried in seal oil with garlic powder sprinkled on top and had it with two leftover pancakes. Very good! Thanks, Natives from Klemtu.

Tried going for a poo at twilight but only managed one tiny pellet."

Five days later, at the Denny Island camp, Billy wrote that he was ready to wrap up his trip, after four months and 20 days.

> Lots of low thunderhead type clouds over the mainland, the bottoms of which seemed to extend right to the ground (later I heard it was fog; the lower part anyway). They were coming very slowly from the northeast. Tide near or at low-water slack. Few moskitoes and no-see-ums around. Looked good to travel. Had enough of the bugs. Got a good smokey fire going to keep them away as I packed up and broke camp.

Nearing Idol Point, he had another unexpected interaction:

> Few small boats trolling just off the point. Looked to be lots of high thin cloud towards the west which was slowly getting closer. Ring around the sun at times. Getting sore and tired time I reached small islands just before Dryad Point lighthouse. And who should I meet just off the point — Andrea and a friend of Bryan's up on vacation, out trolling. It was like a couple of years ago when I met Stewart there. Andrea radioed Bryan to let him know I was back.
>
> Had everything moved part way up the beach by the time Bryan and the kids showed up. Was quite a welcoming committee as Bryan's friend plus Roger (a local) showed up as well. Had supper (plus lots of

beer and talk) with them before moving everything down to the camp which was just the way I had left it. Was twilight time I was done, with the moon partly showing very low to the south-southeast. Was a very long day to end the trip on.

Only a few months later, Billy embarked on his next major trip. This time, it prompted only one journal entry, dated March 20: "Arrive back from five-month trip." He didn't know it yet, but Billy had entered the final year of his life.

Chapter 20

GOING TO GOSLING

The lay of the land was unfamiliar — peculiar, even, the
way it is in dreams — and his destination was unclear. But
he knew he was trying to find something.
—BEN GADD, RAVEN'S END

AFTER RETURNING HOME IN MARCH 2003,
Billy filled in his calendar every day with his where-
abouts, activities, the weather and his meals. In April,
he mostly painted and ate pizza. By the end of the
month, he'd made $240. On May 1, he dug out some
ground for an outhouse and burned garbage. On April
4, he put *Ayak* onto racks and recorded heavy hail. He
spent most of his days painting. On the 7th, he phoned
his friends Darrell and Jan Tom to chat about the painting called *Hole in the Wall* that he was making for them.
On the 9th, he read *Voyage of the Narwhale* by Andrea
Barrett. On the 19th he finished *Hole in the Wall* and
was paid $2,700 for it. Andrea Clerx helped deliver it.
Billy phoned a few days later to confirm the Toms were
happy. The following day, Billy started painting *Full*
Moon on a three-quarter sheet of watercolour paper for
Andrea and Bryan.

At the start of June, he was getting ready for his next trip. He bought supplies, ate pizza, built up his grub-stake and went for hikes. On the 14th, he sat for a video interview with Bryan. "Ran into Kayak Bill, he's been out since March," Bryan began. "He just disappears then shows up out of nowhere. He will go for six months and disappear into the woods. And he is a great artist. Got the eagle feathers on the front of the boat, he just lives on the ocean, amazing guy." Then he asked about Billy's diet, starting with seal meat.

Bryan: What did you do with it? I've never eaten seal.

Billy: So you skin the skin off the blubber, then you skin the blubber off the meat, then you cut the blubber into these little cubes, but about an inch in a cube is about as small as you can go before it's too slippery. Then you put it in a frying pan and it just fills up with oil. And it tastes just like bacon fat.

Bryan: Do you eat that oil?

Billy: Oh, yeah. You put a shot in chapati dough, and a shot in your stew or pancakes. You use it like a butter. You oil your rifle, anything, your tools, knife, anything that would rust. The meat I chop into chunks to fit into my big pot right there. And you boil it until the meat falls off the bone and you can't tell the difference between it and really tender beef. You have to boil it to get the oils out. Then you take the meat and use your hands to make hamburger patties. Then you smoke-dry them, smoke-dried seal burgers. I have about 40 of them right now. All you do is put them in a container of water, right, and they bloat right back up again. Then you make a stew or whatever and then you have three to five gallons of oil.

Bryan: What do you do with it?

Billy: I bring it with me in my kayak, it doesn't last as long as grease, it lasts as long as bacon fat. If you had it in a refrigerator it would be okay. I've got a bottle now and it's still okay and it was made... well, I'd have to check my journal. I was out there for like an infinity.

Bryan: How long were you out there?

Billy: Time is a way different thing out there. A month out there would be like six months here.

Bryan: So you're just living off the land, right?

Billy: It's a Garden of Eden out there. The wild vegetables. Wild peas, carrots, goose tongue and sea asparagus. Five minutes every morning I pick a bag this full of them. It's the sprouts. The peas form these big sprouts, like a bud. You just pick those; they taste just like peas. The carrots the same thing. Goose tongue is just like string bean and sea asparagus like exactly like asparagus. They grow along the high-tide line, they just like to get washed with the sea water. They're huge and you just use that in your cod stew or whatever. And it's really good. Mussels, gooseneck barnacles, the abalone or the clam. The mussels are huge, only six in my big pot. You have to know how to do it right. You have to pull out the five-star mussel which makes the mussel steak — good if you can't find codfish. They're incredible.

Bryan: No McDonald's, eh.

Billy: You'd be amazed at what's washed up over the years. Two years ago, a big plastic container washed up and inside were about 12 cubes vacuum-packed in aluminum, and it was halva.

Bryan: What about deer?

Billy: And yeah, deer, I don't really like shooting them but I will.

From food, the conversation turned to the distances Billy had paddled.

Billy: The longest day I had was 70 miles. That was Sooke to Port Renfrew. I was practising to see if I could cross the Hecate Strait. So I went and did it, but it was ideal conditions, right, it was in the spring with a full-moon tide. I was coming in with monstrous groundswell, like 20 feet, or I don't know how big, but they were hills, smooth as glass. So, you're just going up a hill and Sombrio beach would go by and it was going all the way up. I left at sunrise on June 21 and I set at sunset. I just wanted to know if I could do it.

I have a lot of intermediate camps, so I don't have to do those long ones. I have them all the way up and all the way down. I look for a place in a 25-mile run that would make a good camp. Just a ridge pole and fire pit and a drying rack and a stash bucket with a candle and lighter and some firewood under something. If I'm leaving camp and have a partially empty Bic, I'll just stash it in the bucket. So anyone who is shipwrecked there will find everything. Every camp

has a zigzag sign, that's my mark. Stewart Marshall
says I look like the guy on the Zig-Zag [tobacco label].

Bryan took a moment to adjust the camera ("Billy's
drinking a beer," he said out of frame) before asking
about family life.

Bryan: You named your son Westerly, is that true?
That's not gossip, eh?

Billy: Yeah, I named him Westerly. It's when the
nicest weather is. That was an epic when he was
born. Tried to have him at home first. It was a southeast storm, we got flown out of Echo Bay by a friend.
He's a character. He has a feather growing out of
his back, he lives to fly. And he's huge. He lives in
Mitchell Bay. He flew us out. He lived on a barge in
Echo Bay. A bunch of hippie families, that's where I
met him. He was one of them. I'd never seen anyone
so obsessed with flying.

Brian: Back in the 1960s?

Billy: Yeah, something like that.

*   *   *

On June 18, Billy climbed back into *Ayak* and left
Shearwater for four months. "Denny Island Camp.
Too windy to continue. Wild view of a moonrise very
early with orcas," he wrote. At the end of the month,
"Wet with mod. Southerlies. Moskitoes pretty bad.
Hiked around complete Is. Found new mussels' bed

(big ones)." He ended the month moving from his bivy at Spiller Inlet to his Dallas Island camp and on to Higgins Passage.

In July, he paddled to Aristazabal III, where he lived for a few days before heading to Harvey Island. He stayed busy hiking there and on Byers Islands, and catching cod. He kept note of how many mice he ate, the density of the blackflies, the direction of the wind, the size of his poo, the taste of oysters and the two Zodiacs loaded with people in bright yellow suits that motored pass the north side of the island. On the 18th, he recorded that he took some photos. He drew small pictures of the sun.

August was more of the same, but with more notes about his poo, which was getting larger. There were big gale winds, patchy fog afternoons and beautiful sunsets. Every day, Billy would write three-word sentences into the day-squares on his calendar; the most important notes were circled. As the days went on, his notes became tighter, with clearer handwriting. More acronyms, more arrows and more weather reports.

On Thursday, September 4, he ate his 54th mouse and burned through his sixth candle. On the 27th, he left Aristazabal for the last time and paddled to Higgins Passage, where he heard a lot of wolves howling. He then had a "perfect traveling day along Swindle Island shore" from his Higgins Passage camp to Dallas Island.

By now, he had been out for nearly four months and was making many stops along the way back to Shearwater. On October 4, he paddled 4.5 nautical miles to Cockle Bay on Lady Douglas Island and stopped at a small southeast-facing cabin owned by the Heiltsuk First Nation but open to use by passersby. Billy hadn't stayed in it much before, but a strong low-pressure system was approaching. The cabin provided shelter and bunks for at least 14 people; the main space had a large floor and benches, along with a wood stove big enough to heat the whole cabin, and even a stainless steel sink, but with no running water. An outhouse stood just outside the main building. The morning of October 6 was wet and windy, so he spent the day cooking and doing laundry. It was raining by dinnertime. There's no way to know if Billy slept in a bunk or on the floor near the stove.

The wind and wet weather continued, but Billy paddled out the following day to gather some clams. On the 8th, he wrote that there were storm-force south-easterly winds. The rain lasted 12 hours, and Billy said it was a "wild P.M." The weather calmed over the next few days, and he departed on the 12th for Shearwater. Three wolves sat nearby as he packed *Ayak*. He padded through Perceval Narrows and towards Mathieson Channel and noted "hard paddle thru narrows."

Back in Shearwater, Billy visited stores with Bryan and gave Andrea his camera film to be developed. He spent most of his time packing for his next and final trip, had a "visit from an Englishman" and practised loading *Ayak*. He purchased Drum, a new axe, a grinder and other supplies. On the 4th, he finished a painting for Andrea worth $500. The next day, he wrapped rope around the handle of his new axe. On November 6, the evening before he left, he loaded *Ayak* and then had dinner with Andrea and Bryan. The following day, he paddled away from the shores of Shearwater, never to return.

At Gosling Island, he found his camp had been used. The island is part of the Hakai Protected Area formed in 1985, an archipelago that includes two-thirds of Hunter Island, the northern half of Calvert Island and the Goose Group. The Heiltsuk First Nation are the closest inhabitants to the protected area.

Over the next 30 days, Billy didn't write about anything out of the ordinary. The day after he arrived, an old wooden boat stopped out front, and the day after that a boat with hunters anchored close by. Then, 12 days later, two men hunting out of a punt stopped to chat. A punt is a flat-bottomed boat with a squared bow, often used in small river or shallow water. Over the next few days, the weather cooled, and Billy was visited by a number of deer. From December 1 to 7, he went through two pouches of Drum and started a third. It rained a lot. The only other journal entry that would raise an eyebrow is from December 6, when, after a week involving long hikes and a lot of work around the camp, he wrote about "lower back + stomach pains."

His final journal entry was on the 7th. He wrote a few small notes and then made a tiny dash, next to which he intended to write something. In his hundreds of journals over 40 years, it was the first time he didn't finish an entry. At some point, between then and March, he was shot in the head.

An Elder from Bella Bella, whose wife would sometimes bake bread for Billy, had a feeling that something was wrong on Gosling. Under a dark sky, he took his boat to Billy's camp. There was no smoke billowing from the trees. He pointed his boat south into the bay. The waves lapped onto the beach as the Elder nosed his boat onto shore. "Billy?" he shouted into the bush. Much of the coastline was storm-threatened, and Billy's camp was in disarray. The man returned home and notified the authorities. The RCMP visited Gosling Island and found Billy's body under some driftwood.

It appeared Billy was preparing to pack his belongings to leave camp. His fishing rod and gaffing hook were lashed to *Ayak*. The rudder was up and tied down. His knife was gone — its sealskin sheath was hanging in a tree, mouldy and rotting. A stainless steel cooking pot was full of old fish. His .22 rifle was found nearby.

The RCMP brought most of Billy's belongings back to Shearwater along with his body, but not his kayak. Lori and Westerly didn't understand why and were told the boat was no longer seaworthy. They organized for an RCMP boat in the area to pick it up, and then a friend brought it to Sointula. *Ayak* was in perfect condition. Westerly asked the RCMP where his dad's knife was, but it never turned up. Lori wanted to visit Gosling Island, but no one in Shearwater would take her. Both she and Westerly left Denny Island feeling like they weren't being told everything. "There are some unanswered things, and maybe one day the truth will come out," said Lori. Many people who knew Billy from Shearwater just wouldn't respond when asked about his final months.

After returning home, Lori remembered that she had seen an old man paddling north in a wooden boat in December. She recalled thinking it was her old logging-camp boss, the one who Billy punched out to save her. Rumours over the years had suggested that the man had never given up his grudge against Billy. The thought made her shudder.

Climbers from Calgary, like Perry Davis, Urs Kallen and Gary Jennings travelled to Sointula for Billy's memorial. Urs hadn't seen Billy for 25 years. They met Westerly, Lori and many of Billy's friends, including

Stewart Marshall. It was the first time Billy's climbing friends met his west coast family.

The post-mortem said that Billy had been dead for only around six weeks, even though his final journal entry was written three months before his body was found. It also revealed that no toxins were present in his blood when he died. His rotting teeth were not bad enough to poison him. We'll never know if Billy was alone on his final day or if someone else was with him. Paddler Glenn Lewis said to me, "Wild animals live about half as long as domestic animals. It's just the wear and tear on the body."

Billy had mentioned to his friends over the years that people had fired guns at him; he took these as warning shots not to return. Stewart confirmed that the same thing had happened to him while he was paddling alone near the Goose Group. The bullets from shore rained down near his kayak. He paddled hard to get away.

"If Billy wanted to knock himself out, he would have just paddled out and done it," said Stewart. "There'd be no kayak, no nothing. That's how Billy would have done it."

We don't know what happened at the end of Billy's life. But we do know that the personality Stewart describes — paddling out and doing something, moving forward to the next adventure, conquering the next peak — was the essence of Billy Davidson. As Billy himself wrote, describing the culmination of one of his hardest climbs:

> I feel happy, then suddenly lonely. I somehow feel
> very isolated amongst all this rugged beauty. The
> sun, now just dipping below the mountains to the

west, sends out lines of gold threaded with orange and purple hues... We climb for the moment, and the special enjoyment gained from that moment. Looking back and remembering will never be the same as the original experience. If it were, we should just sit by the fire for the rest of our lives; sipping beer, smoking and just remembering. Instead we climb on and on, searching out those most precious moments wherever they may be found.

EPILOGUE

Alpinism is the art of climbing mountains by confronting the greatest dangers with the greatest prudence... You cannot always stay on the summits. You have to come down again. So, what's the point? Only this: what is above knows what is below, what is below does not know what is above... There is an art to finding your way in the lower regions by the memory of what you have seen when you were higher up. When you can no longer see, you can at least still know.

—RENÉ DAUMAL

STEWART, TWIRLING BILLY'S PAINTBRUSH between his fingers, watched the rising tide. Billy had been gone for 15 years. Stewart told me that he spends most of his days just looking out through the window. The first kayak he ever built hung from beams behind me. It was covered with a layer of sawdust from wood-worms burrowing through the timber above. He hit his fist on the counter. "Damn." He'd been telling me his theories about how Billy died.

With a sore back, a teenage daughter and his art studio gone, Stewart said that his adventuring days were in the past. Walking back to my van, he talked about spending time in the Rockies and asked if we could go on a climb one day. He handed me a clove of garlic from his garden to deliver to Lori. He stood on the road waving goodbye until I was out of sight.

I walked around the ferry deck, watching boats and other passengers. Some of them looked as old as Billy would have been. I wondered how many of them had similar stories about survival in the mountains and on the ocean. I wondered if any of them had crossed paths with Billy.

I opened an email I received from Ingmar Lee, a Bella Bella environmentalist and paddler.

> All I know is that he was found dead on the Goose Islands. I've heard it was suicide, that he was suffering from an extreme toothache and would not deal with the medical system, but there's also rumours that he was murdered. I never met him, we got here a few years after he was gone, but I have visited a few of his sites and appreciate what he did.

Ingmar's words were similar to those of almost everyone I spoke to along the coast.

Since Billy's first few paddling trips in the 1970s, kayakers had set out on expeditions to find him. He became known as the legendary Kayak Bill, and sightings were talked about in pubs. Few if any paddlers who went looking for him ever crossed his path. After his death, Urs Kallen and Perry Davis made a short film featuring Billy's climbing. Accompanying their narration was Billy's synthesizer music. Kayaking magazines started to feature Billy's exploits. In 2005, *Sea Kayaker* published Neil Frazer's "Looking for Kayak

Bill" and Keith Webb's "Kayak Bill — A Requiem." One of Billy's paintings appeared on the cover of *The River Killers* by Bruce Burrows in 2011. In a 2012 *Sea Kayaker* issue, Alex Sidles wrote about Billy in his article "The Dilemma of Solitude."

No one was more of an expert about Billy's west coast camps than Jon Dawkins, a Seattle-based kayaker. After learning about Billy in 2005, he worked for months tracking down Billy's camps with help from Glenn Lewis, Neil Frazer and others. To them, Billy was a paddling guru and inspiration as to how to live simply. Over the years, they repaired many of Kayak Bill's camps. They're not alone. A growing number of west coast paddlers are seeking Billy's camps and retracing his journeys. The camps are tucked away, hidden by bush and above changing tide lines. To paddle to them all — especially alone — would surely make for the adventure of a lifetime.

From Port McNeill, I drove south to Nanaimo to visit Westerly and his wife, Kirsti. They met each other growing up in Sointula. The first time I visited them, Westerly showed me photos from when he lived on the float house. He flipped through his dad's edition of *The Lord of the Rings*. Unlike the well-preserved and annotated sea charts, the book showed signs of heavy use.

Westerly said that one of the things that bothered him the most about the circumstances surrounding his father's death was that his dad's knife was never found.

I asked Westerly if he had thought about following in Billy's wake and going on long solo kayaking adventures. With Kirsti listening intently, Westerly said, "I've thought about it, and maybe I could. And just maybe one day I will."

I visited Lori in the BC interior, where she'd moved with Bob to care for her mom. She and Bob missed watching the tides and living on the west coast. On their living room wall were some of Billy's paintings. I gave her the clove of garlic from Stewart and continued to the Rockies.

The CMC still gets together every few weeks for beers, but it was at Urs's Calgary home that I met him after my trip to the coast. He handed me letters Billy had written him in the 1970s. He then poured us wine and took out an old journal containing photos of mountains with lines scribbled on them — dates, and names of old friends. He turned to a page where Billy had jotted a list of mountain walls he wanted to climb. It was easy to see why they appealed to him. Billy never did climb all of the walls he wanted to. Tucked into a corner at the bottom of the page, he had written, "till the long day is done."

The first time Urs and I had climbed together was on Yamnuska shortly after I learned about Billy. I had never climbed Red Shirt, and Urs wanted to share his tips and tricks with me. It was his 25th ascent of the route in 40 years. He once videotaped Billy and Jeff Horne climbing it. At the base of the climb, Urs pointed to where Billy lit a smoke and slung his hammer. Along the route, he showed me the cracks where Billy hammered in pitons or where they stopped to record. Urs laughed on one ledge and said it was where Billy and Jeff stopped to eat a candy bar for the camera.

I went on to climb dozens of big rock routes and ice climbs with Urs over the years. With information he gave me, I went on to climb almost every route Billy established or climbed during his time in the mountains.

Where the rock revealed a small in-cut for my fingers, I often wondered if Billy had used the same reveal or if he had found a different place to pull himself up. On top of Yamnuska, Urs said, "If you want to climb hard climbs, you have to climb with good guys." He said Billy was one of the best. That's why they climbed such hard routes together.

I stopped in the parking lot below Yamnuska on my drive back to Canmore from Calgary. There was a skiff of fresh snow on the ground, and I was alone. The line where the peaks met the sky was burnt orange, above it purple and black. Ravens climbed into the evening above Yamnuska. I looked at the places where climbers had gone, where Billy had gone, tracing lines up shadowy corners. Coloured leaves dropped in a rush of wind as the rock wall began to fade from sight. The tiny specks in the sky were suddenly gone behind clouds over summits. I watched as the alpenglow gave way to night, and the mountains disappeared into darkness.

ACKNOWLEDGEMENTS

This book would not have been possible without the support of my family and friends. Chic Scott introduced me to the story of Billy, and Urs Kallen was a guiding light throughout the years. Without Urs I would never have been privy to so much intimate knowledge of Billy. Lori Anderson offered important insight into life on the west coast in the 1980s and her relationship with Billy. Without Westerly's blessings and stories, I would never have worked to complete this project. Countless others helped along the way, from Gary Jennings and Perry Davis to Jon Dawkins, Frankie Dwyer, Stewart Marshall and Glenn Lewis. Author David Smart's suggestions helped me focus the narrative year after year. Thanks to Don Gorman and Rocky Mountain Books for giving me the time and feedback required for the book. Thank you to everyone who helped along the way. Most of all, thanks to Billy for living a life that will ultimately inspire many generations.

FURTHER READING

Chouinard, Yvon. *Some Stories: Lessons from the Edge of Business and Sport.* Ventura, Cal.: Patagonia, 2019.

Dornian, Dave, Ben Gadd and Chic Scott. *The Yam: 50 Years of Climbing on Yamnuska.* Calgary: Rocky Moutain Books, 2008.

Dwyer, Francis. *Passing Innocence.* Victoria: Trafford, 2002.

Long, John. *The Stonemasters: California Rock Climbers in the Seventies.* Santa Barbara: T. Adler Books / Stonemaster, 2009.

McLane, Kevin. *Squamish: The Shining Valley*, rev. ed. Squamish: High Col, 2020.

Miller, Robert H. *Kayaking the Inside Passage: A Paddling Guide from Olympia, Washington, to Muir Glacier, Alaska.* Woodstock, Vt.: Countryman, 2005.

Scott, Andrew. *Painter, Paddler: The Art and Adventures of Stewart Marshall.* Victoria: Touchwood, 2003.

Tabei, Junko, and Helen Y. Rolfe. *Honouring High Places: The Mountain Life of Junko Tabei.* Translated by Yumiko Hiraki and Rieko Holtved. Calgary: Rocky Mountain Books, 2017.

Turner, Nancy. *Plants of Haida Gwaii*, 3rd ed. Madeira Park, BC: Harbour, 2021.

Wood, Rob. *Towards the Unknown Mountains.* Campbell River, BC: Ptarmigan, 1991.

INDEX

D

Dallas Island, 22, 199, 200, 205, 207–8

Davidson, Billy, 5, 12; "Dollar Bill," 190; Kayak Bill, 177, 183, 184; "William (Acid) Davidson," 127; "William Lighthead," 130

Davidson, Ken, 12, 18, 183

Davidson, Kirsti, 228

Davidson, Westerly, 3, 9, 175–76, 178, 182–83, 185, 194, 199, 202, 219, 223, 228

Davis, Perry, 3, 118, 168, 186, 187, 223, 227

Dawkins, Jon, 228

Denny, Glen, 81

Denny Island, 8

Denny Island Camp, 219

Desolation Sound, 152

Discovery Islands, 154

Discovery Mountain, 168

Dixon, Mount, 102

Dolt Tower, 83

Don Peninsula, 206

Donegal Head. *See* Malcolm Island, Donegal Head

Dowd, John, 176

Doyle, Kevin, 167

Drury Inlet, 174

Dryad Point, 203, 213

Dufferin Island, 199, 200, 203

Dufferin Island Camp, 208

Duncan, 194

Dwyer, Francis, 13

Dwyer, Frankie, 13–15

Dyson, George, 158, 188

E

East Redonda, 153

Echo Bay, 170, 172, 174–75, 181, 194, 219

Eden Island, 169, 199

Edith Cavell, Mount, 77, 167

Edmonton, 71

Eisenhower Tower, 21–22

Eisenhower Youth Hostels, 21

El Capitan, 52, 81; Nose, the, 81; Dolt Tower, 83; Outer Space, 83; Shield, the, 118; Snow Creek Wall, 83; Stoneman Meadow, 83; Triple Cracks, 118; Zodiac Wall, 118

Elbow River, 17

Elder (Bella Bella), 222

Elzinga, Jim, 103, 120–22, 167

Empress, The, 73, 78, 92, 103, 118, 126, 155, 166

Engelke, Simpson, 18

Engelke, William, 18

Esther Point, 181

Evans, Tom, 82

Evans Point, 170

Extended Point, 183

F

Faint, Joe, 77

Fay, Mount, 46

Feuerer, Bill "Dolt," 81, 83

Finlayson Channel, 184

Firth, Jack, 2, 66, 73, 124, 126

Fisherman Bay, 189

Fox Group islands, 169

Fraser Valley, 148

Frazer, Neil, 227, 228

Frost, Tom, 80, 84, 87

Furtin, John, 65

G

Gale Passage, 201, 205

Gallwas, Jerry, 111

Gardner, Don, 48, 59

Gaudette, Edmond, 187

Georgia Strait, 154